Easy Japanese Phrases

Over 1700+ Phrases for Effortless Communication in Japan | A Comprehensive and Up-to-Date Guide for Quick Learning and Memorable Experiences

SORA TAKAI

SORA TAKAI

COPYRIGHT OF THE SORA TAKAI 2024

Contents

Preface vii

Part 1
1. Introduction to Japanese Pronunciation

1. 2. BASIC GRAMMAR OVERVIEW 7
   - Sentence Structure 7
   - Particles and Their Uses 10
   - Verbs and Tenses 12
2. 3. NUMBERS, DATES, AND TIME 15
   - Counting in Japanese 15
   - Days of the Week and Months 18
   - Telling Time and Date Formats 20

Part 2
4. Greetings and Introductions

3. 5. COMMON COURTESIES AND POLITE EXPRESSIONS 31
   - Please and Thank You 31
   - Apologies and Excuses 33
   - Respectful Language 34
4. 6. EMERGENCY AND HEALTH-RELATED PHRASES 37
   - Asking for Help 37
   - Medical Emergencies 38

Part 3
7. Shopping and Transactions

5. 9. DIRECTIONS AND TRANSPORTATION 51
   - Asking for and Giving Directions 51
   - Public Transportation 52
   - Renting Vehicles 53

6.	10. ACCOMMODATION AND LODGING	55
	Hotel Check-In and Check-Out	55
	Room Types and Amenities	56
	Requests and Complaints	57
7.	11. SOCIALIZING AND LEISURE ACTIVITIES	59
	Invitations and Arrangements	59
	Sports and Hobbies	60
	Nightlife and Entertainment	61
8.	12. EXPRESSING OPINIONS AND FEELINGS	63
	Likes and Dislikes	63
	Agreement and Disagreement	64
	Expressing Emotions	65

Part 4
13. Business and Formal Interactions

9.	14. TECHNOLOGY AND COMMUNICATION	71
	Using Phones and Internet	71
	Social Media Phrases	72
	Technological Terms	73
10.	15. CULTURAL AND FESTIVAL EXPRESSIONS	77
	Traditional Festivals in Japan	77
	Cultural Landmarks in Japan	78
	Understanding Japanese Historical and Religious Terms	81

Part 5
16. Tips for Effective Communication in Japan

11.	17. CULTURAL NOTES AND TABOOS	91
	Understanding Japanese Etiquette	91
	Navigating Social Situations in Japan	92
	Cultural Dos and Don'ts in Japan	95
12.	18. REGIONAL VARIATIONS IN LANGUAGE	99
	Dialects and Accents	99
	Understanding and Adapting:	100
	Understanding Regional Slang and Idioms	100
	Embracing Local Customs and Phrases	101

Afterword

Preface

Introduction to the Japanese Language

As we set forth on the exploration of the Japanese language within this phrasebook, it's essential to recognize the unique characteristics and nuances that make Japanese a fascinating subject of study. Unlike many Western languages, Japanese presents a tapestry of linguistic structures, sounds, and cultural contexts, all intertwined in a way that shapes not just communication, but also the very fabric of social interaction.

At the heart of the Japanese language is its deep connection to Japan's rich cultural heritage. Every phrase and expression carries with it a history and a set of expectations about politeness, respect, and the subtleties of Japanese etiquette. For instance, the language distinguishes itself through various levels of politeness, from the casual speech often used among friends to the highly respectful forms reserved for formal situations or when addressing someone of higher status. This aspect of the language is not just about grammar or vocabulary; it's a reflection of the societal values of respect and humility.

The structure of the Japanese language also offers a window into its complexity and beauty. Comprising three scripts – Hiragana, Katakana, and Kanji – it challenges learners to embrace a system of writing that is both pictorial and symbolic. Hiragana, with its flowing, cursive style, is used for native Japanese words and grammatical elements. Katakana, more angular in

Preface

appearance, often represents foreign words and names. Meanwhile, Kanji, borrowed from Chinese characters, conveys not only meaning but also provides clues to pronunciation. This trichotomy is not merely a linguistic feature; it's a testament to Japan's history of cultural assimilation and adaptation.

Furthermore, the phonetic nature of Japanese, with its relatively small range of sounds, may initially seem like a simplification. However, the subtlety lies in the pitch accent, where the same spelling can lead to different meanings based on the tonal variation. This nuance adds a layer of complexity often surprising to new learners.

Japanese is not just a language of communication but also of representation. The language possesses a rich array of onomatopoeic expressions, mirroring the sounds and rhythms of life. These expressions breathe life into the language, allowing speakers to vividly convey emotions, actions, and the natural world in a way that is almost graphic.

Delving into Japanese requires more than just learning words and grammar; it's about immersing oneself in a different way of thinking and expressing. Each phrase and idiom opens a door to understanding the Japanese mindset, where harmony, precision, and the unspoken often carry as much weight as the spoken word. It's a language where what is left unsaid can be as important as what is said, reflecting a culture that values subtlety and implication.

This phrasebook, therefore, is more than just a collection of phrases; it's a guide to navigating the linguistic and cultural landscape of Japan. Whether you are a traveler seeking to enrich your experience in Japan, a student of language and culture, or simply a curious mind, the journey through these pages will offer insights not only into how to speak Japanese but also how to understand and appreciate the intricate tapestry that is Japan.

How to Use This Phrasebook

In creating this phrasebook, our aim is to offer a tool that is not only informative but also intuitive and user-friendly, catering to both novices and those with some familiarity with the Japanese language. Understanding how to effectively utilize this resource will enhance your learning experience, making it both enjoyable and practical.

Preface

The phrasebook is structured to gradually guide you through various aspects of the Japanese language, beginning with fundamental phrases and gradually introducing more complex expressions. Each section is carefully curated to reflect real-life scenarios, providing you with a practical toolkit for communication. This approach ensures that you not only learn the language but also understand its application in everyday contexts.

To maximize the benefits of this phrasebook, it is recommended to approach it with a sense of curiosity and openness. Japanese, with its unique blend of linguistic and cultural nuances, offers a rich learning experience. As you navigate through the pages, try to immerse yourself in the language. Practice the phrases aloud, paying attention to pronunciation and intonation, which are crucial in Japanese communication.

Additionally, this book is designed to be a quick reference in various situations. Whether you are in a restaurant trying to order food, at a train station needing directions, or in a shop making a purchase, the phrasebook provides easy access to relevant sections. This design is particularly useful for travelers who need to communicate effectively while on the move.

One of the key features of this resource is its focus on cultural context. Japanese language is deeply intertwined with the culture, and understanding this interplay is essential for effective communication. Throughout the book, you will find cultural notes and tips that provide insights into Japanese etiquette and social norms. These snippets of information are not just trivia; they are integral to understanding how and when to use certain phrases.

Remember, language learning is a journey, not a destination. It involves making mistakes, asking questions, and gradually building confidence. This phrasebook is your companion in this venture, offering support and guidance as you explore the beautiful and complex language of Japan.

As you use this phrasebook, allow yourself the freedom to explore, experiment, and engage with the language in a way that suits your learning style and needs. Whether you are planning a trip to Japan, studying the language for personal enrichment, or simply indulging in a love for languages, this phrasebook is designed to be a reliable and enriching guide on your linguistic adventure.

Preface

A Brief Overview of Japanese Culture and Etiquette

As we venture into the realm of the Japanese language with this phrasebook, it is imperative to recognize that language and culture are inextricably linked. The Japanese language is not just a means of communication; it is deeply rooted in the cultural and social fabric of Japan. Understanding these cultural nuances is crucial for anyone looking to engage with the language meaningfully.

Japanese culture is renowned for its emphasis on respect, harmony, and politeness. These values permeate every aspect of life in Japan, from everyday interactions to the language itself. In Japan, communication is often indirect, with much left unsaid, relying on context and non-verbal cues to convey meaning. This indirectness is a reflection of the value placed on maintaining harmony and avoiding confrontation.

One of the most distinctive aspects of Japanese culture is the concept of 'wa' or harmony. This principle governs social interactions, ensuring a smooth and harmonious flow in relationships. It is essential to understand this concept as it influences the way you should use the phrases in this book. For example, directness or bluntness in speech is often avoided, and there is a significant emphasis on reading the atmosphere ('kuuki wo yomu') to understand unspoken expectations.

Another important aspect is the hierarchical structure of Japanese society. Respect for seniors and those in higher positions is deeply ingrained in the culture. This respect is reflected in the language through different levels of politeness and honorifics. Understanding when to use polite or humble language is not just a matter of linguistic competence but also cultural sensitivity.

In addition to these overarching cultural themes, there are numerous etiquettes and customs that one should be aware of. For instance, bowing is a common way to greet, thank or apologize. The depth and duration of the bow convey the level of respect or sincerity. Gift-giving is another important aspect of Japanese culture, with specific rules regarding how and when to give and receive gifts.

Furthermore, Japanese culture places great importance on group harmony over individual desires. This collectivist mindset affects interactions and

Preface

decision-making processes. In a group setting, consensus and the well-being of the group are prioritized over individual opinions.

It is also worth noting that Japanese culture is rich in traditions and rituals, many of which are tied to the changing seasons. From cherry blossom viewing in spring to New Year celebrations, these cultural events offer a glimpse into the heart of Japan and its people.

Part 1

1. Introduction to Japanese Pronunciation

Vowels and Consonants

In embarking on the study of Japanese pronunciation, it is essential to start with the foundational elements of the language: vowels and consonants. These are the building blocks of Japanese speech, and their correct pronunciation is crucial for clear and effective communication.

Japanese vowels are distinct in their clarity and consistency. The language consists of five vowels: 'a,' 'i,' 'u,' 'e,' and 'o.' Each vowel has a single, pure sound, unlike in English where vowels can have multiple sounds. The vowel 'a' is pronounced as 'ah' like in 'father,' 'i' as 'ee' in 'see,' 'u' as 'oo' in 'food,' 'e' as 'eh' in 'met,' and 'o' as 'oh' in 'go.' The purity of these vowel sounds is a defining characteristic of Japanese pronunciation, lending a melodic quality to the language.

The consonants in Japanese, while somewhat familiar to English speakers, also have their unique aspects. One of the most notable features is the absence of strong consonant sounds as in English. For example, the Japanese 'r' is a sound somewhat between the English 'r' and 'l,' pronounced with a light tap of the tongue near the roof of the mouth. Another point to note is that certain consonant sounds, such as 'si,' are pronounced more like 'shi,' and 'ti' as 'chi.'

Japanese also does not have consonant clusters like in English. Instead, almost every consonant is followed by a vowel, creating a rhythmic and fluid sound to the language. This characteristic makes Japanese relatively easier to pronounce once the basic sounds are mastered.

The consonants 'g,' 'z,' 'd,' and 'b' can be slightly nasal in certain contexts, a subtle feature that can be picked up through listening and practice. Additionally, the consonants 'k,' 's,' 't,' and 'p' are pronounced more softly than in English, without a strong burst of air.

Understanding and mastering these vowel and consonant sounds is the first step towards fluency in Japanese. It is through these sounds that one can begin to form the simple yet elegant words and phrases that are characteristic of the Japanese language. Regular practice, attentive listening, and immersion in spoken Japanese are key to developing a clear and accurate pronunciation, laying a solid foundation for further exploration of this beautiful language.

One of the unique features of Japanese consonants is the presence of voiced and voiceless sounds. For instance, 'k' and 'g' are pairs where 'k' is voiceless and 'g' is voiced. Similarly, 's' and 'z,' 't' and 'd,' and 'p' and 'b' form such pairs. This distinction is crucial as it can change the meaning of words. For example, 'kami' can mean paper (with a voiceless 'k') or god (with a voiced 'g'). This subtle yet significant aspect of Japanese pronunciation requires careful attention and practice.

Another key aspect is the pronunciation of the 'h' sound in Japanese, which can vary. In some regions and contexts, it is pronounced softly, almost like a gentle exhalation. However, in other instances, especially when it precedes certain vowels, it can take on a more pronounced, almost 'f'-like quality.

The Japanese language also includes double consonants, known as 'sokuon.' This is where a consonant sound is held slightly longer, creating a brief pause before the next vowel. This feature can be heard in words like 'kitte' (stamp) and 'kitta' (cut), where the double 't' creates a distinct pronunciation difference that can alter the meaning.

It is also essential to understand that while Japanese has fewer sounds than many other languages, the way these sounds are combined and used in context can convey a variety of expressions and emotions. The rhythm and pitch in which these sounds are spoken play a significant role in Japanese communication. Unlike English, where stress is placed on certain syllables to convey meaning, in Japanese, variations in pitch (high or low) across the vowels in a word can change its meaning.

The journey of mastering Japanese pronunciation is not just about learning individual sounds but also about understanding their interaction and flow within words and sentences. Listening to native speakers, practicing spoken Japanese, and immersing oneself in Japanese media can greatly enhance this learning process.

As you continue to familiarize yourself with these vowel and consonant sounds, remember that patience and persistence are key. The initial challenge of adapting to these new sounds will gradually lead to a more natural and confident use of the language, opening up a new world of communication and cultural understanding.

Pitch Accent and Intonation

Venturing further into the nuances of Japanese pronunciation, we encounter the subtle yet pivotal elements of pitch accent and intonation. These aspects of spoken Japanese are not just linguistic features; they are the essence that brings the language to life, imbuing it with emotion, nuance, and clarity.

Pitch accent in Japanese is a means of distinguishing words through variations in pitch. Unlike in English, where stress is placed on certain syllables to change the meaning of words, Japanese uses a combination of high and low pitches. Every syllable in Japanese can be pronounced with either a high or low pitch, and the pattern of these pitches can alter the meaning of a word. For example, the word 'hashi' can mean 'bridge' when pronounced with a high pitch on the first syllable and a low pitch on the second, or 'chopsticks' when pronounced with the opposite pattern. This feature of Japanese makes it crucial for learners to attune their ears to these pitch variations to understand and be understood correctly.

Intonation, on the other hand, is about the rise and fall of pitch across entire phrases or sentences. It conveys emotions and attitudes and is deeply linked to the context in which words are spoken. The intonation of a sentence can express doubt, certainty, surprise, or a question, even without changing the words used. For instance, a rising intonation at the end of a sentence typically indicates a question in Japanese, similar to English.

It's important to note that pitch accent patterns can vary regionally within Japan. While standard Tokyo dialect, often taught in educational contexts, has its own distinct pitch accent rules, other regions in Japan may have different patterns. This diversity adds richness to the language, although it can also pose an extra layer of complexity for learners.

Mastering pitch accent and intonation requires attentive listening and practice. Immersing oneself in Japanese spoken by native speakers – through conversations, movies, and other media – is an effective way to develop an intuitive understanding of these aspects. It is also helpful to practice speaking aloud, ideally with feedback from native speakers, to fine-tune your pronunciation.

Common Pronunciation Challenges

As learners delve into the world of Japanese pronunciation, they often encounter a series of challenges that, while initially daunting, offer opportunities for deeper understanding and mastery of the language. These hurdles are not just obstacles to overcome, but gateways to a more nuanced and authentic grasp of Japanese.

One of the primary challenges faced by learners, especially those from Western linguistic backgrounds, is the subtle distinction in sounds that do not exist in their native languages. For instance, the Japanese 'r' sound, as mentioned earlier, is an amalgamation of the English 'l,' 'r,' and 'd' sounds, and mastering this requires a keen ear and practice. It involves a light tap of the tongue against the alveolar ridge, which can be quite unfamiliar to new learners.

Another common challenge is the differentiation between long and short vowel sounds. In Japanese, the length of a vowel can change the meaning of a word entirely. For example, 'obaasan' (grandmother) and 'obaasan' (old woman) differ only in the length of the vowel 'a'. This aspect of Japanese pronunciation demands careful attention to duration and rhythm in speech.

Consonant sounds in Japanese also present their hurdles. The 'tsu' sound, for instance, is not native to many languages and can be tricky to articulate. It requires a combination of 't' and 's' sounds made almost simultaneously, which is a unique articulatory process for many learners.

The concept of 'sokuon,' or the double consonant, poses another challenge. It requires a momentary pause before the following consonant, a feature that is crucial in differentiating words but can be difficult to master without practice.

Additionally, the pitch accent and intonation patterns, as previously discussed, are fundamental to effectively communicating in Japanese. These are not just about the correct pronunciation of words but also about conveying the right emotion and intention behind the speech.

Overcoming these challenges involves a mix of focused practice, attentive listening, and immersive exposure to the language. It is beneficial for learners to engage regularly with native speakers and Japanese media, which can greatly enhance their understanding and pronunciation skills.

It's important for learners to approach these challenges with patience and persistence. Mispronunciations and mistakes are a natural part of the learning process. Each challenge overcome adds a layer of depth to the learner's understanding and ability in Japanese, transforming these hurdles into stepping stones towards fluency. Remember, the goal is not just to pronounce words correctly, but to embrace and internalize the unique rhythms and sounds of the Japanese language.

These challenges, when approached with curiosity and persistence, can significantly enhance your understanding and appreciation of the language's unique character.

1. Distinguishing Similar Sounds: Japanese contains pairs of sounds that are subtly different yet crucial to distinguish. A notable example is the difference between は ('ha') and ば ('ba'). While both involve similar mouth positions, ば requires a voiced vibration of the vocal cords. This distinction can be perplexing, as it changes the meaning of words, such as 'hana' (flower) and 'bana' (nose). Practicing with minimal pairs, words that differ only in these sounds, can be a practical approach to mastering these nuances.

2. Perfecting the Japanese 'R': The Japanese 'r' sound, a singular sound somewhere between 'l,' 'r,' and 'd' in English, poses a notable challenge. It's articulated by lightly tapping the tip of the tongue against the alveolar ridge (the roof of the mouth just behind the upper teeth), a motion unfamiliar to many non-native speakers. A useful practice is to say words like 'tara' (codfish) or 'kirei' (beautiful), focusing on the smooth, fluid motion of the tongue.

3. Long vs. Short Vowels: Lengthening vowels appropriately is crucial in Japanese. Mispronouncing 'Ojiisan' (grandfather) with a short 'i' as 'Ojisan' (uncle) might lead to amusing misunderstandings. To practice, try repeating pairs of words, emphasizing the length of vowels, like 'kite' (come) and 'kiite' (listen).

4. Consonant Clusters and 'Sokuon': The 'sokuon' or double consonant, where a tiny pause is followed by a sharp consonant sound, is unique to Japanese. Words like 'kakkoii' (cool) and 'itte' (saying) are examples. To get the hang of this, practice speaking phrases like 'pocchitto' (a little bit), paying attention to the slight stop between the consonants.

5. Mastering 'Tsu': The 'tsu' sound, as in 'tsunami,' is not native to many languages. It's formed by placing the tongue close to the roof of the mouth, almost as if pronouncing a 't,' then quickly transitioning to an 's' sound. Practice with words like 'kutsu' (shoes) to refine this.

6. Dealing with Voiced and Unvoiced Consonants: In Japanese, certain consonants have both voiced and unvoiced versions. For instance, 'k' (unvoiced) and 'g' (voiced) as in 'kaku' (to write) and 'gaku' (to learn). Understanding this distinction is vital for accurate pronunciation. A helpful exercise is to alternate between words that use these sounds, like 'sora' (sky) and 'zora' (slang for sky).

7. Pitch Accent and Intonation: The melody of the language, conveyed through pitch accent and intonation, can be elusive. The word 'ame' can mean rain (with a flat or falling pitch) or candy (with a rising pitch). Listening to native speech and mimicking the pitch patterns can be incredibly helpful. Watching Japanese shows or listening to songs and trying to replicate the intonation patterns can accelerate this learning.

8. Nasal Sounds: Some Japanese sounds are slightly nasal, especially 'n' at the end of words or before 'b' and 'p' sounds. This can be practiced with words like 'kanban' (signboard) and 'tempura' (a type of Japanese dish).

In overcoming these challenges, the key is to immerse oneself in the language. Listening to and mimicking native speakers, whether through media, conversation exchanges, or language apps, is invaluable.

Chapter 1
2. Basic Grammar Overview

Sentence Structure

Embarking on the study of Japanese grammar, particularly its sentence structure, is an intriguing venture into the language's unique logic and arrangement. The structure of Japanese sentences can be quite different from English, yet understanding these differences is key to grasping the language's essence and communicating effectively.

Japanese follows a Subject-Object-Verb (SOV) sentence structure, in contrast to the Subject-Verb-Object (SVO) structure commonly used in English. This means that in Japanese, the verb typically comes at the end of the sentence. For example, whereas in English one would say "I eat sushi," in Japanese, it translates to "Watashi wa sushi o tabemasu" (I sushi eat). This structure is a fundamental aspect of Japanese grammar and is consistent across simple and complex sentences.

In Japanese, particles play a crucial role in sentence construction. These are small words that follow nouns and verbs, indicating their function in the sentence. For instance, 'wa' is a topic marker, 'ga' is a subject marker, 'o' is an object marker, and 'ni' can indicate direction or location. Understanding and using these particles correctly is crucial for clear communication.

Another aspect of Japanese sentence structure is the flexibility in omitting the subject when it's understood from the context. This aspect often makes

Japanese sentences seem vague to English speakers. For example, "Gakkou ni ikimasu" can mean "I go to school," "He goes to school," or "They go to school," depending on the context.

The use of adjectives and adverbs in Japanese also differs from English. In Japanese, adjectives can directly modify the nouns they describe without needing a linking verb. Additionally, adjectives have to agree with the tense of the sentence, something not seen in English. For example, "Kirei na hana" means "beautiful flower," where 'kirei na' is the modifying adjective.

Questions in Japanese are formed simply by adding 'ka' at the end of a statement. For instance, "Anata wa gakusei desu" (You are a student) becomes "Anata wa gakusei desu ka?" (Are you a student?) when 'ka' is added at the end.

Moreover, the concept of politeness and formality is deeply embedded in Japanese sentence structure. Different verb forms are used depending on the level of politeness or formality required by the situation. For example, the casual form of the verb "to do" is 'suru,' while the polite form is 'shimasu.'

Lastly, the use of honorifics and humble forms of speech reflects the hierarchical nature of Japanese society. These forms alter the sentence structure to show respect or humility, and they are an integral part of formal and polite Japanese speech.

This exploration is not merely an academic exercise but a practical guide to understanding how ideas and information are organized and conveyed in Japanese.

1. Subject-Object-Verb Order: The foundational structure of Japanese sentences is the Subject-Object-Verb (SOV) order. This arrangement is quite different from the Subject-Verb-Object (SVO) order commonly used in English. For instance, the English sentence "I read a book" translates to "Watashi wa hon o yomimasu" in Japanese, literally "I book read." This structure is consistent in Japanese, whether in simple, everyday speech or complex, formal writing.

2. Role of Particles: Japanese particles are small yet powerful words that follow nouns and verbs, indicating their role in a sentence. Understanding particles is crucial for constructing sentences correctly. For example, 'wa' (は) designates the topic of the sentence, 'ga' (が) identifies the subject, 'o' (を) marks the direct object, and 'ni' (に) is used for indicating direction, location, or indirect objects. These particles are essential in giving sentences clarity and direction.

3. Implicit Subjects: Unlike English, where the subject is often explicitly stated, Japanese sentences frequently omit the subject when it is clear from the context or previous conversation. This feature can initially confuse learners, but it adds to the subtlety and efficiency of the language. For instance, saying "Eiga o mita" can mean "I saw a movie," "He saw a movie," or "We saw a movie," depending on the context.

4. Adjective-Noun Agreement: In Japanese, adjectives can directly modify nouns without needing additional linking verbs. Furthermore, adjectives must agree with the tense and politeness level of the sentence. This alignment is a unique feature not present in English. For example, "kirei na hana" (beautiful flower) uses a present-tense adjective, while "kirei datta hana" (was a beautiful flower) uses a past-tense adjective.

5. Forming Questions: Japanese questions are formed by adding 'ka' (か) at the end of a statement. This simplicity in question formation is one of the more straightforward aspects of Japanese grammar. For example, "Kore wa nan desu ka?" translates to "What is this?" in English.

6. Politeness and Verb Forms: Japanese verbs change form to reflect varying levels of politeness. The casual form of a verb is used among friends or in informal settings, while the polite form is employed in more formal or respectful contexts. For example, the verb 'iku' (to go) in its polite form becomes 'ikimasu'. This aspect of sentence structure is pivotal in Japanese, reflecting the cultural importance of respect and hierarchy.

7. Honorific and Humble Forms: Japanese also employs honorific and humble forms of speech. These forms alter sentence structure to show respect or humility. Understanding when and how to use these forms is essential for effective communication, especially in formal settings.

8. Practical Application: To practice Japanese sentence structure, it's helpful to start with simple sentences and gradually incorporate more complex elements. Writing and translating short paragraphs, engaging in conversation with native speakers, or using language learning apps are practical ways to apply these concepts.

9. Listening and Imitation: Regularly listening to and imitating native speakers is invaluable. This practice helps learners internalize the rhythm, flow, and structure of Japanese sentences, moving beyond textbook examples to real-life application.

10. Patience and Persistence: Remember, mastering Japanese sentence structure takes time and patience. Mistakes are part of the learning process and provide opportunities for improvement. With consistent practice and exposure, learners can develop a strong understanding and appreciation for the elegant structure of Japanese sentences.

Particles and Their Uses

Venturing into the intricacies of Japanese grammar, one cannot overlook the pivotal role played by particles. These small yet significant elements are integral to the language, guiding the flow of sentences and clarifying the relationships between words. Understanding their uses and nuances is essential for anyone seeking to communicate effectively in Japanese.

1. 'Wa' (は) - The Topic Marker: Perhaps the most fundamental particle in Japanese, 'wa' marks the topic of the sentence, distinguishing it from the subject. It is used to introduce what is being talked about and sets the stage for the rest of the sentence. For example, in "Sakura wa kirei desu" (The cherry blossoms are beautiful), 'sakura' is the topic being discussed.

2. 'Ga' (が) - The Subject Marker: While 'wa' indicates the topic, 'ga' is used to highlight the subject, especially when introducing new information or emphasizing a specific subject. In the sentence "Kare ga sensei desu" (He is a teacher), 'kare' is emphasized as the subject.

3. 'O' (を) - The Direct Object Marker: This particle is used to mark the direct object of a verb, indicating what the action is being done to. In "Hon o yomimasu" (I read a book), 'hon' (book) is the direct object of the action 'reading.'

4. 'Ni' (に) - Direction or Indirect Object Marker: 'Ni' is a versatile particle used to indicate a direction, point in time, or an indirect object. For example, "Gakkou ni ikimasu" (I go to school) shows direction, while "Kanojo ni tegami o kaku" (I write a letter to her) indicates the recipient of the action.

5. 'De' (で) - The Context Marker: This particle is used to set the context, such as location or means. In "Toshokan de benkyou shimasu" (I study at the library), 'toshokan' (library) is the location where the studying takes place.

6. 'No' (の) - The Possessive or Modifier Particle: 'No' is used to indicate possession or to modify a noun with another noun. For instance, "Watashi no kuruma" means "my car," where 'no' shows ownership.

7. 'Kara' (から) and 'Made' (まで) - Indicating Range: These particles are used to indicate the range of action or time. 'Kara' means 'from,' and 'made' means 'until.' For example, "Getsuyoubi kara kin'youbi made" (From Monday to Friday).

8. 'To' (と) - The Conjunctive Particle: Used to list items or to indicate accompaniment, 'to' functions similarly to 'and' in English. In "Ringo to banana o kau" (I buy apples and bananas), it lists items being bought.

9. 'Mo' (も) - The Inclusion Particle: Equivalent to 'also' or 'too' in English, 'mo' is used to include something or someone in the action. "Kare mo kimasu" translates to "He is also coming."

10. 'Ka' (か) - The Question Marker: Placed at the end of a sentence, 'ka' turns a statement into a question, akin to the English question mark. For example, "Kore wa nan desu ka?" means "What is this?"

Grasping their uses can be like unlocking a code, revealing the deeper meaning and structure of the language.

1. 'Ne' (ね) - Seeking Agreement or Confirmation: This particle is often added at the end of a sentence to seek agreement or confirmation, similar to saying "right?" or "isn't it?" in English. For example, "Atsui desu ne?" translates to "It's hot, isn't it?"

2. 'Yo' (よ) - Asserting Information: When you want to assert something or present information that you believe is new to your listener, 'yo' is used. It's like adding "I tell you" for emphasis in English. For example, "Kore wa oishii yo" means "This is delicious, I tell you."

3. 'Tte' (って) - Quoting or Informal Topic Marker: This informal particle is used for quoting someone or something informally. It's like saying "said" or "like" in English. For example, "Kanojo wa 'ureshii' tte" translates to "She said she's happy" or "She's like 'I'm happy.'"

4. 'Soshite' (そして) - Connecting Sentences: While not a particle in the traditional sense, 'soshite' functions similarly to 'and' in English, connecting sentences or ideas. For example, "Kinou eiga o mita. Soshite, resutoran ni itta" means "Yesterday, I watched a movie. And then, I went to a restaurant."

5. 'Demo' (でも) - Contrasting or Offering Alternatives: This word is used to introduce a contrast or an alternative, akin to "but" or "however" in English. For example, "Samui desu. Demo, soto ni ikimasu" translates to "It's cold. But, I'm going outside."

6. 'Nagara' (ながら) - Doing Two Things at Once: 'Nagara' is used to indicate doing two things simultaneously, like saying "while" in English. For example, "Aruki nagara, tabemasu" means "I eat while walking."

Understanding these particles in Japanese is like putting together pieces of a puzzle. Each particle has its place and role, helping to shape the overall picture of the sentence. Using these particles correctly can bring your Japanese from simple to more natural and fluent.

Verbs and Tenses

When you start learning Japanese, one of the coolest things you'll discover is how verbs and tenses work. Unlike English, where you have to remember a lot of different verb forms, Japanese keeps things a bit simpler. Let's dive into this fun part of the language that brings action to your sentences!

1. Verb Basics: In Japanese, verbs come at the end of a sentence. Cool, right? For example, in English, you say, "I eat sushi." In Japanese, it's "Sushi o tabemasu" – literally, "Sushi eat." Japanese verbs don't change depending on the subject. Whether it's "I eat," "she eats," or "they eat," the verb stays the same: "tabemasu."

2. The Magic of Verb Forms: Japanese has something super interesting: the verb form stays the same no matter who's doing the action. But, it changes based on the tense (like past or present) and the level of politeness. Two main forms are the polite form (like "tabemasu") and the plain form (like "taberu"). The polite form is like adding a "please" to make it sound nicer.

3. Present and Future Tense: Guess what? In Japanese, you use the same tense for both present and future actions. For example, "tabemasu" can mean "I eat" or "I will eat." The context lets you know whether it's happening now or later.

4. Past Tense – Just Add 'ta': To talk about things you did, just change the end of the verb. For polite form, "tabemasu" (eat) becomes "tabemashita" (ate). For plain form, "taberu" becomes "tabeta." It's like adding "-ed" in English but simpler!

5. Negative Form – Saying 'No' to Actions: To say you don't do something, tweak the verb a bit. "Tabemasu" (eat) turns into "tabemasen" (do not eat) for the polite form. In plain form, "taberu" becomes "tabenai." It's handy for saying what you don't like or don't do.

6. Let's Have Fun with Verbs: The best way to get these verb forms down is to use them in fun ways. Try making sentences about stuff you love or your daily routine. Like "Every morning, coffee o nomimasu" (I drink coffee). Or talk about your hobbies, "Weekends ni, eiga o mimasu" (I watch movies on weekends).

7. Listening and Repeating: A super cool trick is to listen to how people speak in Japanese shows or songs. You'll hear how they use verbs in real life. Try repeating after them. It's like learning to dance by following the steps of a pro dancer!

In Japanese, verbs are like the engine of a car – they keep your sentences running. And once you get the hang of these forms, you'll be zipping through conversations like a race car driver on a track. Remember, practice makes perfect, and soon you'll be using verbs like a pro!

Let's keep exploring this exciting part of Japanese, using super easy words and ideas that are simple to understand.

1. Te-Form – The Swiss Army Knife of Verbs: One of the coolest things in Japanese is the 'te-form' of verbs. Think of it as a magic wand that can change a verb to do different things. You use it to ask someone to do something, to say "let's do," or to link actions together. For example, "Tabete kudasai" means "Please eat," and "Asobi ni ikimashou" (Let's go play) uses the te-form of 'iku' (to go).

2. Connecting Actions – Like Linking Train Cars: The te-form is awesome for connecting actions, just like linking train cars. Say you want to say, "I wake up, eat breakfast, and go to school." In Japanese, you'd use the te-form like this: "Okite, asagohan o tabete, gakkou ni ikimasu." It's a smooth way to talk about doing one thing after another.

3. The Cool Part about 'Want to do': To say you want to do something in Japanese, just add "tai" to the verb. Like "tabetai" means "want to eat." It's super handy for expressing your desires and wishes, like "I want to see a movie" or "I want to visit Japan."

4. Expressing 'Can do' and 'Cannot do': In Japanese, you can easily say if you can or cannot do something. Just change the verb a bit. For example, "Taberareru" means "can eat," and "Taberarenai" means "cannot eat." It's great for talking about your abilities or things you're not able to do.

5. It's All About the Context: Remember how the same verb form can mean present or future? That's where context comes into play. The words around the verb and the situation you're in make it clear. If you say "Asu, sushi o tabemasu" (Tomorrow, I will eat sushi), we know it's about the future because of "asu" (tomorrow).

6. Practicing with Fun Sentences: The best way to get comfy with verbs and tenses is to make sentences about stuff you like or do. Say things about your favorite foods, places, or hobbies. For example, "Mainichi, neko to asobimasu" (Every day, I play with my cat).

7. Easy Does It: Learning verbs and tenses in Japanese is like learning to ride a bike. At first, it might seem tricky, but once you get it, it's like, "Wow, I'm doing it!" So, take it easy, practice a bit every day, and soon you'll find it's not as hard as it seemed.

In Japanese, verbs are like the paintbrushes of language. They let you paint pictures of what you do, what you like, and what you want to do. So, have fun with them, play around, and watch your Japanese conversations become more colorful and lively!

Chapter 2
3. Numbers, Dates, and Time

Counting in Japanese

Counting in Japanese is like unlocking a secret code that's both simple and fun. You might think numbers are just numbers, but in Japanese, they take you on a cool adventure. Let's jump into this world of numbers and see how they work in the Japanese language.

1. Basic Numbers - The Building Blocks: Japanese numbers start easy. Just like building blocks, you learn the basic numbers and then stack them up to make bigger ones. Let's look at one to ten: 'ichi' (1), 'ni' (2), 'san' (3), 'shi' or 'yon' (4), 'go' (5), 'roku' (6), 'shichi' or 'nana' (7), 'hachi' (8), 'kyuu' (9), and 'juu' (10). These are your main tools for counting.

2. Making Bigger Numbers - Just Add Up: To make bigger numbers, you just add these basic numbers together. For example, eleven is 'juu-ichi' (10 + 1), and twenty-two is 'ni-juu-ni' (2 x 10 + 2). It's like a fun puzzle or a math game.

3. Hundreds and Thousands - More Fun with Numbers: For hundreds, you say 'hyaku,' and for thousands, it's 'sen.' So, 300 is 'san-byaku' and 2000 is 'ni-sen.' Notice something cool here? The way you say 'three hundred' changes a little from 'san' (three) to 'san-byaku.' It's like giving the number a little twist to make it fit just right.

4. Big Numbers - They Have Cool Names Too: When you get into really big numbers, they have special names. Ten thousand is 'man,' and a hundred million is 'oku.' Imagine you're counting stars; you'd use these big number names!

5. Counting Different Things - Special Words Alert: Japanese has something special called 'counters.' They are like tags you add to numbers when counting different things. For example, for counting flat things like paper, you say 'ichi-mai,' 'ni-mai,' and so on. It's like saying "one sheet of paper," "two sheets of paper" in English, but with a special twist.

6. Practice Makes Perfect - Let's Count Everything: The best way to get good at Japanese numbers is to count everything around you. Count your steps, the cars on the street, or the stars in the sky. Say the numbers out loud in Japanese, and soon you'll be counting like a pro.

7. Fun with Numbers - They're Everywhere: Numbers are everywhere – in your phone number, address, on the calendar, and even when you go shopping. Pay attention to these numbers in your daily life, and try to think of them in Japanese. It's a fun way to learn!

In Japanese, counting isn't just about numbers; it's a way to connect with the language and see the world in a new way. Every number you learn is a step further in your adventure with Japanese. So, keep counting and have fun with every number you meet!

It's like exploring a treasure island where every number is a new discovery.

1. Counting Past 100 - Bigger Adventures: Once you're comfortable with smaller numbers, the adventure gets even bigger. Let's say 100 ('hyaku'), 1,000 ('sen'), and 10,000 ('man'). For bigger numbers, you just combine these with the smaller numbers. For instance, 150 is 'hyaku-go-juu' (100 + 50), and 2,500 is 'ni-sen-go-hyaku' (2,000 + 500). It's like putting pieces of a puzzle together.

2. Special Changes - A Twist in the Tale: Some numbers change a bit when combined with 'hyaku,' 'sen,' and so on. Like 'san-byaku' (300) instead of 'san-hyaku,' or 'roppyaku' (600) instead of 'roku-hyaku.' It might sound like a tongue twister, but it's actually pretty cool once you get the hang of it.

3. Counting Objects - A Japanese Specialty: Remember the special 'counters' we talked about? There are many of them, depending on what you're counting. For animals, use 'hiki' (like 'ippiki' for one animal), for long objects like pencils or trains, use 'hon' ('ippon' for one), and for books, use 'satsu' ('issatsu' for one). It's like giving each object its own special number word.

4. Days of the Month - Not Just Ordinary Numbers: When you say the dates in Japanese, it gets a bit unique. The first day of the month is 'tsuitachi,' not 'ichi-nichi.' The 20th is 'hatsuka,' and some days like the 14th ('juu-yokka') sound different too. It's like each day of the month has its own personality.

5. Years in Japanese - Counting Time: For years, you use the regular numbers plus 'nen' for year. Like 2021 is 'ni-sen-ni-juu-ichi-nen.' It's fun to think about what each year number means in Japanese, like a journey through time.

6. Counting Fun - Make It a Game: Turn counting into a game. How fast can you count to 100 in Japanese? Can you name the days of the month in order? Challenge your friends or family, and make it a fun competition.

7. Everyday Practice - Numbers Are Your Friends: Look for numbers in everyday life – on TV, in books, when you're cooking (measuring ingredients), or setting your alarm. Try to think of these numbers in Japanese. It's a great way to make friends with numbers in Japanese.

There's so much more to explore and enjoy:

1. Beyond 10,000 - Reaching for the Stars: In Japanese, numbers can go really high. After 'man' (10,000), you have 'juu-man' (100,000), 'hyaku-man' (1,000,000), and even 'oku' (100,000,000). Imagine counting all the stars in the sky, and you're using these big numbers!

2. Age-Specific Counters - Special Birthday Numbers: In Japan, there are special counters for age. For example, 'issai' for one year old, 'ni-sai' for two years old, and so on. Knowing these helps you say your age like a native speaker.

3. Telling Time - It's About Hours and Minutes: Telling time in Japanese is fun. Hours are counted with 'ji,' like 'ichi-ji' (1 o'clock), and minutes with 'fun' or 'pun,' like 'san-juppun' (30 minutes). So, 3:30 is 'san-ji san-juppun.' It's like putting together pieces of a time puzzle.

4. Traditional Japanese Counting - A Glimpse into History: There's also a traditional way of counting things in Japanese, like using 'ko' for small objects ('ikko,' 'niko'), 'mai' for flat objects ('ichimai,' 'nimai'), and 'hon' for long cylindrical objects ('ippon,' 'nihon'). It's a peek into how things were counted in olden times.

5. Money Matters - Counting Yen: When talking about money, you use 'en' for yen. So, 100 yen is 'hyaku-en,' and 5,000 yen is 'go-sen-en.' It's handy when you go shopping or talk about prices.

6. Counting Steps - A Healthy Habit: A fun way to practice is by counting your steps in Japanese. When you walk or exercise, count each step like 'ichi, ni, san...' It's a great way to practice numbers and stay healthy.

7. Japanese Number Rhymes and Songs: Just like in English, there are rhymes and songs in Japanese that help children (and adults too!) learn numbers. They're catchy, fun, and a great way to get those numbers stuck in your head.

8. Practice, Practice, Practice: The key to mastering Japanese numbers is practice. Use them as often as you can – when you cook (measuring ingredients), at the store, or just counting random things around you. The more you use them, the more natural they become.

Counting in Japanese isn't just a skill; it's a window into a different way of seeing the world. Every number tells a story and connects you more deeply with the Japanese language and culture. So keep counting, and enjoy every number as a step on your journey through the beautiful world of Japanese.

Days of the Week and Months

Now, let's have some fun learning about the days of the week and months in Japanese. It's like discovering a new set of cool words that help you talk about your plans, birthdays, and holidays!

1. Days of the Week - Easy as a Song: The days of the week in Japanese are super fun to learn. Each day ends with 'youbi,' which means 'day.' It starts with 'getsuyoubi' (Monday), which sounds like 'moon day.' Then comes 'kayoubi' (Tuesday), 'suiyoubi' (Wednesday), 'mokuyoubi' (Thursday), 'kinyoubi' (Friday), 'doyoubi' (Saturday), and 'nichiyoubi' (Sunday). It's like a weekly song!

2. Remembering the Days: A cool way to remember these is to think of little stories. Like, "getsu" sounds like 'get,' so imagine getting started with the week on 'getsuyoubi.' And 'nichi' in 'nichiyoubi' sounds like 'niche,' so think of Sunday as a special 'niche' day for rest.

3. Months of the Year - A Number Game: Months in Japanese are super easy because they're just numbers. January is 'ichigatsu' (one month), February is 'nigatsu' (two month), and so on, up to December, which is 'juunigatsu' (twelve month). It's like counting, but with months!

4. Talking About Dates - Mix and Match: When you talk about dates, you just mix the day and month. Like, 'juugatsu juuyokka' (October 14th). It's like putting puzzle pieces together – one for the month and one for the day.

5. Seasons in Japanese - Nature's Palette: The seasons in Japanese are 'haru' (spring), 'natsu' (summer), 'aki' (autumn), and 'fuyu' (winter). Each season has its own charm, like cherry blossoms in 'haru' and colorful leaves in 'aki.'

6. Practice Makes Perfect - Use It in Conversation: The best way to get good at days and months is to use them when you chat. Talk about your birthday, like "Watashi no tanjoubi wa shichigatsu nanoka desu" (My birthday is July 7th), or make plans like "Raishuu no kayoubi ni aimashou" (Let's meet next Tuesday).

7. Fun with Calendars and Diaries: If you have a calendar or diary, try labeling them in Japanese. It's a great way to see these words every day and get used to them.

8. Celebrations and Holidays: Learn about Japanese holidays and how they're tied to dates and seasons. It's a cool way to connect with Japanese culture and practice your new words.

Let's explore even more about the days of the week and months in Japanese, turning each day and month into a fun and interesting part of your language adventure.

1. Days of the Week – A Closer Look: Each day of the week in Japanese has a cool background. They're named after elements like the sun, moon, and five elements (water, wood, metal, fire, and earth). For example, 'nichiyoubi' (Sunday) comes from 'nichi,' which means 'sun.' Imagine the sun shining on a relaxing Sunday!

2. Fun with Month Names: Remembering month names in Japanese is like playing with numbers. 'Ichigatsu' (January) is like saying 'Month One,' 'nigatsu' (February) is 'Month Two,' and so on. It's a number game that takes you through the whole year!

3. Special Dates - Mark Your Calendar: In Japan, certain dates have special significance. For example, 'tanabata' (Star Festival) is celebrated on July 7th, or 'shichigatsu nanoka.' Learning about these special dates is a fun way to connect with Japanese culture.

4. Seasons and Months – A Natural Connection: Each season in Japan is rich with cultural traditions and natural beauty. 'Haru' (spring) is famous for cherry blossoms, making March (san-gatsu) and April (shi-gatsu) special. 'Aki' (autumn) brings stunning fall colors, making October ('juugatsu') and November ('juuichigatsu') beautiful months to enjoy nature.

5. Using Days and Months in Daily Life: Try talking about your favorite seasons or months in Japanese. Say things like "Haru ga suki desu" (I like spring), or "Juugatsu ni kouyou o mi ni ikimasu" (I will go to see autumn leaves in October). It's a great way to practice and share your interests.

6. Birthdays and Anniversaries: Use your knowledge of days and months to talk about birthdays and anniversaries. For example, "Watashi no tanjoubi wa rokugatsu juunika desu" (My birthday is June 12th). It makes these occasions more fun and personal.

7. Planning Events – Let's Hang Out: Invite friends out or plan events using the days and months. "Raishuu no doyoubi ni eiga o mimashou" (Let's watch a movie next Saturday), or "Hachigatsu ni natsu yasumi ga arimasu" (I have a summer break in August). It's a practical and enjoyable way to use your Japanese.

8. Days of the Week and Months in Songs and Stories: Japanese children learn days and months through songs and stories, and so can you! Look for children's songs or simple stories in Japanese that mention days and months. They're catchy and make learning super fun.

Understanding the days of the week and months in Japanese opens up a world of conversation about time, schedules, and events. It helps you plan, share, and enjoy life's moments, both big and small. So, keep practicing these words, use them in your daily life, and watch how they bring a special Japanese flavor to your days and months!

Telling Time and Date Formats

Now, let's have a blast learning about telling time and date formats in Japanese. It's like getting the keys to a secret code that helps you plan fun activities, remember special days, and never be late for an exciting event!

1. Telling Time - It's a Fun Puzzle: In Japanese, telling time is like putting together a puzzle. You say the hour first, then add 'ji' for hour, and then the minutes. For example, 3:15 is 'san-ji juugo-fun.' Think of it as saying "three hour fifteen minutes." It's a different way of telling time, but it's really fun once you get used to it.

2. AM and PM - A Simple Twist: To say AM and PM, you add 'gozen' for AM (like 'gozen hachi-ji' for 8 AM) and 'gogo' for PM (like 'gogo ichi-ji' for 1 PM). It's like saying "morning eight hour" and "afternoon one hour." Pretty simple, right?

3. Date Formats - A New Way to Mark Days: In Japanese, dates are usually written year first, then month, and then day. So, March 10th, 2021, is written as '2021-nen san-gatsu tooka.' It's like saying "Year 2021, Month 3, Day 10." It's a logical way to think about dates.

4. Special Time Expressions - For Everyday Chat: Japanese has cool ways to say things like 'today,' 'yesterday,' and 'tomorrow.' 'Kyou' (today), 'kinou' (yesterday), and 'ashita' (tomorrow) are super useful in daily conversation. Imagine telling your friend, "Kyou, eiga o mimashou" (Let's watch a movie today).

5. Birthdays - Celebrate in Japanese Style: To say your birthday in Japanese, you start with the month, then the day, and then say 'tanjoubi.' If your birthday is April 9th, you'd say 'shi-gatsu kokonoka tanjoubi.' It's a fun way to share your special day with friends.

6. Planning Events - Using Dates and Time: When planning events or making appointments, use your new skills in telling time and dates. Say things like "Raishuu no kayoubi, gogo san-ji ni" (Next Tuesday at 3 PM). It's practical and makes you sound like a pro.

7. Seasons and Months - Connecting Time with Nature: Japanese culture connects time closely with nature. Learn about how different months and seasons are celebrated. For example, 'hanami' (flower viewing) in spring, or 'momijigari' (autumn leaf viewing) in fall. It brings a poetic touch to how you see time and seasons.

8. Practice Makes Perfect - Talk About Time and Dates: The best way to get good at this is to talk about time and dates in Japanese as much as you can. Discuss plans, birthdays, holidays, or what you did 'kinou' (yesterday). The more you use it, the more natural it becomes.

Learning to tell time and understand dates in Japanese is not just about being punctual; it's about connecting with the culture, making plans, and enjoying every moment. It turns every appointment and special day into a fun language adventure. So, keep practicing, and soon you'll be talking about time and dates like a native speaker!

Let's delve even deeper into the captivating world of telling time and understanding date formats in Japanese. It's like unlocking more secrets of this beautiful language!

1. Half Hours and Quarter Hours - Adding Variety: Just like in English, you can express half hours and quarter hours in Japanese. For half past, you add 'han' after the hour, like 'san-ji han' (3:30). For quarter past or to, use 'juugo-fun' (15 minutes) or 'sanjuu-fun' (30 minutes). Imagine saying, "It's quarter past two" as 'ni-ji juugo-fun.'

2. Days of the Month - Special Words to Remember: Days of the month in Japanese have some unique expressions. The 1st of the month is 'tsuitachi,' the 2nd is 'futsuka,' the 3rd is 'mikka,' and so on. These special terms are like little keys to unlock each day of the month.

3. Years in Japanese - Talking About Eras: In Japan, years can also be expressed in eras based on the reign of the emperor. For example, the Reiwa era started in 2019. 'Reiwa ni-nen' is 2020 in this era. It's a fascinating way to connect time with history.

4. Expressing Duration - How Long Things Take: To talk about how long something takes, use 'kan' or 'jikan.' For example, 'san-jikan' (three hours) or 'ni-kan' (two days). It's useful when you're planning activities or talking about travel.

5. Using Time Expressions in Conversations: When chatting in Japanese, sprinkle in time expressions. Talk about your routine, like "Maiasa gozen roku-ji ni okimasu" (I wake up at 6 AM every morning), or share your plans,

"Konshuu no nichiyoubi ni kaimono ni ikimasu" (I will go shopping this Sunday).

6. Holidays and Festivals - Celebrating Japanese Style: Learn about Japanese holidays and festivals and how they're tied to specific dates. For example, 'Oshogatsu' (New Year's) is a big celebration in 'ichigatsu' (January). Talking about these events helps you practice dates and brings you closer to Japanese culture.

7. Fun with Timers and Alarms - Practice Every Day: Set timers or alarms on your phone or watch in Japanese time format. It's a great daily exercise to reinforce your learning and get used to hearing and seeing time in Japanese.

8. Interactive Learning - Games and Apps: Use language learning apps and games that focus on time and dates. They make learning fun and interactive, and you get to practice in a playful environment.

Mastering the ways of telling time and understanding dates in Japanese is like adding new colors to your language palette. It enhances your ability to plan, remember, and celebrate special moments.

Part 2
4. Greetings and Introductions

Basic Greetings

Greetings are like the open doors to new friendships and experiences. In Japanese, they're simple, friendly, and full of respect. Let's step into the world of Japanese greetings, where every 'hello' is a smile in words!

1. The Classic Hello - こんにちは **(Konnichiwa)**: This is the most famous Japanese greeting. It's like saying "Good day" or "Hello." Use it from late morning to early evening. It's perfect for almost every casual situation.

2. Good Morning - おはようございます **(Ohayou Gozaimasu)**: This is how you say "Good morning" in a polite way. If you're talking to friends or family, you can just say "おはよう (Ohayou)." It's like a cheerful way to start the day.

3. Good Evening - こんばんは **(Konbanwa)**: When the day turns to night, switch to "Konbanwa" to greet people. It's a nice way to acknowledge the evening, whether you're entering a restaurant or meeting someone for a night out.

4. Goodbye - さようなら **(Sayounara)**: This is a formal way to say "Goodbye." It's often used when you won't see someone for a while. It's like a respectful way to part ways.

5. See You Later - じゃあね (Jaa ne): For a more casual or informal goodbye, you can say "Jaa ne." It's like saying "See ya!" among friends. It's light and friendly.

6. Thank You - ありがとうございます (Arigatou Gozaimasu): Gratitude is big in Japan. "Arigatou Gozaimasu" is a polite way to say "Thank you." With friends, just saying "ありがとう (Arigatou)" is cool.

7. Excuse Me/Sorry - すみません (Sumimasen): This word is super useful. Use it to get someone's attention, apologize, or even thank someone informally. It's like a Swiss Army knife of politeness.

8. Introducing Yourself - 名前は...です (Namae wa... desu): When meeting new people, just say your name followed by "です (desu)," which is like saying "is." For example, "Namae wa Anna desu" means "My name is Anna." It's a simple and friendly way to introduce yourself.

9. How Are You? - お元気ですか (Ogenki desu ka?): This is a polite way to ask someone how they're doing. It's not used as casually as in English, but it's a nice phrase to know.

10. Responses to Greetings - Simple and Sweet: When someone says "Ohayou Gozaimasu," reply with the same. For "Konnichiwa" and "Konbanwa," just repeat the greeting back. It's like an echo of friendliness.

Introducing Oneself

Introducing yourself in Japanese is like opening the door to new friendships and connections. It's simple, polite, and can be quite fun. Let's learn how to share a bit about yourself in a way that's easy and engaging.

1. Sharing Your Name - 名前を教える (Namae o oshieru): Start with your name. You can say "私の名前は [Your Name] です (Watashi no namae wa [Your Name] desu)," which means "My name is [Your Name]." It's straightforward and friendly.

2. Where You're From - 出身地を伝える (Shusshinchi o tsutaeru): Share where you're from with "私は [Your Country] から来ました (Watashi wa [Your Country] kara kimashita)," meaning "I am from [Your Country]." It's a great way to start a conversation about your background.

3. Your Occupation - 職業を紹介する (Shokugyou o shoukai suru): You can mention what you do for work with "私は [Your Occupation] です (Watashi wa [Your Occupation] desu)," like "I am a teacher" or "I am a student." It gives a glimpse into your daily life.

4. Your Hobbies - 趣味について話す (Shumi ni tsuite hanasu): Sharing your hobbies can make the conversation more interesting. Say "私の趣味は [Your Hobby] です (Watashi no shumi wa [Your Hobby] desu)," such as "My hobby is reading" or "My hobby is traveling."

5. Why You're Learning Japanese - 日本語学習の理由 (Nihongo gakushuu no riyuu): If you're learning Japanese, share your reason with "日本語を勉強 しています, なぜなら [Your Reason] (Nihongo o benkyou shite imasu, nazenara [Your Reason])." For example, "I am studying Japanese because I love the culture."

6. Expressing Gratitude for the Meeting - 会えて嬉しいと伝える (Aete ureshii to tsutaeru): Show your happiness to meet someone with "お会いで きて嬉しいです (Oaidekite ureshii desu)," which means "I am happy to meet you." It's a warm and polite expression.

7. Asking About the Other Person - 相手について尋ねる (Aite ni tsuite tazuneru): After introducing yourself, ask about the other person. "あなたにつ いてもっと教えてください (Anata ni tsuite motto oshiete kudasai)" means "Please tell me more about you." It shows that you are interested in them as well.

8. Keeping It Simple and Friendly - 簡単でフレンドリーに保つ (Kantan de furendorii ni tamotsu): Remember, introductions don't have to be long or complicated. Keep them simple and friendly. Smiling and a relaxed attitude can make a huge difference.

let's explore some more simple yet engaging ways to share about who you are and create a friendly atmosphere.

1. Mentioning Your Age - 年齢を話す (Nenrei o hanasu): If it's appropriate, you might want to share your age. Say "私は [Your Age] 歳です (Watashi wa [Your Age] sai desu)," like "I am 20 years old." In Japan, age can be an interesting part of getting to know someone better.

2. Talking About Family - 家族について話す (Kazoku ni tsuite hanasu): If you're comfortable, you can mention your family. "家族は [Number of Family Members] 人です (Kazoku wa [Number of Family Members] nin desu)" means "I have [number] people in my family." It's a nice way to share a bit more about your personal life.

3. Expressing Your Feelings About Japan - 日本に対する感想 (Nihon ni taisuru kansou): Share your feelings about Japan with phrases like "日本が大好きです (Nihon ga daisuki desu)," meaning "I love Japan." It shows your enthusiasm and appreciation for the culture.

4. Your Favorite Japanese Things - 好きな日本のもの (Suki na Nihon no mono): Talk about your favorite Japanese food, place, or tradition. "私は [Your Favorite] が好きです (Watashi wa [Your Favorite] ga suki desu)" can start many interesting conversations.

5. Learning About Each Other - 互いに学ぶ (Tagai ni manabu): After sharing about yourself, encourage the other person to share too. "あなたの趣味は何ですか (Anata no shumi wa nan desu ka?)" means "What are your hobbies?" It's a friendly way to show you're interested in them.

6. Sharing Your Japanese Learning Journey - 日本語学習の旅 (Nihongo gakushuu no tabi): If you're a learner, talk about your Japanese learning journey. "日本語を勉強して [Duration] です (Nihongo o benkyou shite [Duration] desu)" means "I have been studying Japanese for [Duration]." It might inspire an engaging discussion about language learning.

7. Keeping it Light and Positive - 明るくポジティブに保つ (Akaruku pojitibu ni tamotsu): While introducing yourself, keep the tone light and positive. Share things that might spark joy and interest in the conversation.

8. Ending with a Smile - 笑顔で終える (Egao de oeru): As you finish your introduction, do it with a smile. A warm and friendly demeanor can make your introduction memorable and pleasant for the other person.

Introducing yourself is the first step in forming a connection. In Japanese, it's not just about the words you use but also about the warmth and interest you convey. So go ahead, share a little about yourself, ask about the other person, and enjoy the beautiful beginnings of a new friendship or conversation in Japanese!

Responding to Introductions

Responding to someone's introduction in Japanese is as important as introducing yourself. It's about showing interest and respect. Let's look at how you can respond in a way that's easy, friendly, and sure to make a great impression.

Easy Japanese Phrases

1. Acknowledging the Introduction - 紹介に対する反応 (Shoukai ni taisuru hannou): When someone introduces themselves, a simple "はい、了解しました (Hai, ryoukai shimashita)" which means "Yes, I understand," shows you are listening attentively.

2. Expressing Pleasure - 喜びを表す (Yorokobi o arawasu): Respond to their introduction with "あなたに会えて嬉しいです (Anata ni aete ureshii desu)," meaning "I am pleased to meet you." It's a warm way to show you're glad to make their acquaintance.

3. Commenting on Shared Interests - 共通の興味についてコメントする (Kyoutsuu no kyoumi ni tsuite komento suru): If they mention a hobby or interest, respond with "それは面白いですね (Sore wa omoshiroi desu ne)," meaning "That's interesting." It's a nice way to show you're engaged in the conversation.

4. Asking a Follow-Up Question - フォローアップの質問をする (Foroappu no shitsumon o suru): Keep the conversation going by asking a follow-up question like "それについてもっと教えてください (Sore ni tsuite motto oshiete kudasai)," which means "Please tell me more about that." It shows genuine interest in what they have shared.

5. Sharing a Little About Yourself - 自分について少し話す (Jibun ni tsuite sukoshi hanasu): After they have introduced themselves, it's your turn. Share a bit about yourself related to what they said to find common ground.

6. Using Polite Language - 丁寧な言葉を使う (Teinei na kotoba o tsukau): In Japanese culture, using polite language shows respect. Even in casual conversations, maintaining a level of politeness is appreciated.

7. Encouraging a Friendly Atmosphere - フレンドリーな雰囲気を促進する (Furendorii na funiki o sokushin suru): Smile and maintain a friendly tone. Non-verbal cues are as important as your words in creating a pleasant interaction.

8. Wishing to Talk More - さらに話を続けたいと思う (Sarani hanashi o tsuzuketai to omou): End your response with "また話しましょう (Mata hanashimashou)," meaning "Let's talk again," to leave the door open for future conversations.

In responding to introductions, the goal is to create a connection and show that you value the other person. With these simple responses, you can build a bridge of friendship and understanding, paving the way for more delightful interactions in Japanese!

Chapter 3

5. Common Courtesies and Polite Expressions

Please and Thank You

In Japanese culture, politeness and showing respect are very important. This chapter covers the magic words "Please" and "Thank You," which are key in making a good impression. These words are simple yet powerful, showing your manners and respect.

1. Saying 'Please' - 「お願いします」**(Onegaishimasu):** This phrase is like the magic word. Use it when you're asking for something, like "水をお願いします (Mizu o onegaishimasu)" for "Water, please." It makes your request sound polite and respectful.

2. A More Casual 'Please' - 「ください」**(Kudasai):** This is another way to say 'please,' often used after a verb or noun. Like, "これをください (Kore o kudasai)" means "Please give me this." It's friendly and still polite.

3. Expressing Gratitude - 「ありがとうございます」**(Arigatou gozaimasu):** The all-important "Thank you." It's the best way to show appreciation. Whether someone gives you a gift or does something nice, a heartfelt "ありがとうございます" goes a long way.

4. A Casual Thank You - 「ありがとう」**(Arigatou):** This is a more casual form of "Thank you." Use it with friends or in less formal situations. It's friendly and shows that you're grateful.

5. Saying 'You're Welcome' - 「どういたしまして」**(Douitashimashite):** When someone thanks you, reply with "どういたしまして." It means "You're welcome" and shows that you're happy to help.

6. Politeness in Small Things - Small Acts, Big Impressions: In Japan, even small gestures like handing over money or receiving a business card are done with both hands and a nod to show respect.

7. Apologizing Politely - 「すみません」**(Sumimasen):** This word is a polite way to say "I'm sorry" or "Excuse me." Use it if you bump into someone accidentally or need to get someone's attention politely.

8. Showing Gratitude for a Meal - 「いただきます」**and**「ごちそうさまでした」**:** Before eating, say "いただきます (Itadakimasu)" to express gratitude for the meal. After finishing, say "ごちそうさまでした (Gochisousama deshita)" to thank for the food.

Let's delve a bit deeper into these expressions, ensuring they are used accurately and thoughtfully.

9. Expressing Deep Gratitude - 「心から感謝します」**(Kokoro kara kansha shimasu)**: When you want to convey more than just a casual thanks, use "心から感謝します," which translates to "I thank you from the bottom of my heart." It's a sincere way to express deep gratitude.

10. Being Humble with 'Please' - Modesty Matters: When requesting a favor or service, adding a touch of humility can be very effective. For example, "もしよろしければ、手伝っていただけますか？ (Moshi yoroshikereba, tetsudatte itadakemasu ka?)" translates to "If it's okay with you, could you please help me?" This shows respect for the person you're asking for help.

11. Grateful for Understanding - 「ご理解いただき、ありがとうございます」**(Go rikai itadaki, arigatou gozaimasu)**: Use this phrase to thank someone for their understanding, especially in complex or difficult situations. It shows appreciation for their patience and comprehension.

12. Politeness in Requests - Adding Softness: To soften a request, you can use "ちょっとお願いがあるのですが... (Chotto onegai ga aru no desu ga...)," which means "I have a small favor to ask..." This introduction makes your request sound less direct and more polite.

13. The Art of Refusal - Saying No Politely: Directly saying no can be considered rude in Japanese culture. Instead, use "難しいかもしれません

(Muzukashii kamoshiremasen)," meaning "It might be difficult." This indirect way of refusal is seen as more polite and less confrontational.

14. Expressing Apologies for Trouble - 「ご迷惑をおかけして申し訳ありません」 **(Go meiwaku o okake shite moushiwake arimasen)**: This phrase is used to apologize for causing trouble or inconvenience. It's a respectful way to acknowledge your mistake and express regret.

15. Gratitude in Parting - 「お世話になりました」 **(Osewa ni narimashita)**: This phrase is used when leaving a place or at the end of a stay. It means "Thank you for everything," showing appreciation for the care and hospitality received.

16. Remembering Politeness in Emails and Texts: When writing emails or texts, starting with "お疲れ様です (Otsukaresama desu)" and ending with "よろしくお願いします (Yoroshiku onegaishimasu)" adds a layer of politeness and respect to your message.

Apologies and Excuses

Navigating social interactions in Japan often involves understanding the subtleties of apologies and excuses. Let's explore some key phrases that can be used to convey sincerity and respect.

17. Simple Apology - 「ごめんなさい」 **(Gomen nasai)**: This is the basic way to say "I'm sorry" in Japanese. It can be used in casual situations and is a must-know phrase for anyone learning Japanese.

18. Formal Apology - 「申し訳ありません」 **(Moushiwake arimasen)**: For more formal or serious situations, this phrase is appropriate. It translates to "I have no excuse" and shows a deeper level of remorse.

19. Excusing Oneself - 「ちょっと失礼します」 **(Chotto shitsurei shimasu)**: When you need to leave a room or pass by someone, use this phrase. It means "Excuse me for a moment" and is a polite way to interrupt.

20. Apology for Lateness - 「遅れてすみません」 **(Okurete sumimasen)**: If you're late for an appointment or meeting, this phrase is essential. It means "Sorry for being late."

21. Apology for a Mistake - 「間違えました、すみません」 **(Machigaemashita, sumimasen)**: When you've made a mistake, admitting it with this phrase shows humility and responsibility. It means "I made a mistake, I am sorry."

22. Asking for Forgiveness - 「許してください」**(Yurushite kudasai)**: In situations where you seek forgiveness, this phrase is used. It translates to "Please forgive me."

23. Declining Politely - 「残念ですが、できません」**(Zannen desu ga, dekimasen)**: When you need to decline an offer or invitation, use this phrase. It means "Unfortunately, I cannot."

24. Expressing Regret - 「残念に思います」**(Zannen ni omoimasu)**: To express regret or disappointment in a polite way, use this phrase. It shows that you are sympathetic to the situation.

25. Apologizing for Trouble - 「ご迷惑をおかけして、申し訳ありませんでした」**(Go meiwaku o okake shite, moushiwake arimasen deshita)**: This phrase is used to apologize for causing trouble or inconvenience. It's a respectful way to acknowledge your actions and their impact.

Respectful Language

In Japanese culture, showing respect through language is not just important—it's a vital part of daily communication. Here's how to express respect in various situations.

26. Honorific Prefix - 「お」or「ご」**(O or Go)**: These prefixes are added to words to elevate their status. For example, 'tea' (茶, cha) becomes 'お茶' (ocha), showing a higher level of respect.

27. Respectful Address - 「さん」**(San)**: A versatile suffix used after a person's name, 'san' is similar to 'Mr.' or 'Ms.' in English. It's a safe choice in most social interactions.

28. Humble Speech - 謙譲語 **(Kenjougo)**: This form of speech is used to be humble about one's actions. For instance, 'saying' is simply 'いう' (iu), but in a humble form, it becomes '申す' (mousu).

29. Polite Verbs - ます **(Masu) Form:** Verbs in the 'masu' form are polite. For example, 'to eat' (食べる, taberu) in a polite form is '食べます' (tabemasu).

30. Showing Gratitude - 「ありがとうございます」**(Arigatou gozaimasu)**:
A step above 'arigatou', this phrase expresses deeper thanks and is suitable in formal situations.

31. Expressing Understanding - 「承知しました」**(Shouchi shimashita)**:
This phrase means "I understand" and is used to show that you acknowledge and respect the other person's point of view or request.

32. Respectful Request - 「お願いします」**(Onegaishimasu):** When asking for a favor or making a request, this phrase adds a layer of respect.

33. Polite Decline - 「恐れ入りますが」**(Osoreirimasu ga)**: This phrase is used to politely decline an offer or invitation. It literally means "I am afraid" and is a respectful way to say no.

34. Respectful Apology - 「お詫び申し上げます」**(Owabi moushiagemasu)**: A formal way to apologize, especially in business or formal situations.

35. Polite Inquiry - 「お尋ねします」**(O-tazune shimasu)**: Instead of directly asking a question, this phrase is a polite way to inquire about something.

Chapter 4

6. Emergency and Health-Related Phrases

Asking for Help

In situations where you need assistance, especially in a country where your language skills might be limited, knowing the right phrases can be lifesaving. Here's how to ask for help in Japanese in a way that's simple and to the point.

36. Seeking Immediate Attention - 「助けてください」 **(Tasukete kudasai)**: This phrase means "Please help me" and is useful in urgent situations.

37. Reporting an Emergency - 「緊急です！」 **(Kinkyuu desu!):** Use this to alert someone that there's an emergency. It's direct and gets immediate attention.

38. Requesting Medical Assistance - 「救急車を呼んでください」 **(Kyuukyuu-sha o yonde kudasai)**: If you or someone else needs an ambulance, this phrase is crucial.

39. Explaining Symptoms - 「痛いです」 **(Itai desu)**: Simply saying "It hurts" followed by pointing to the area of discomfort can convey a lot to a medical professional.

40. Allergy Alert - 「アレルギーがあります」 **(Arerugii ga arimasu)**: If you have allergies, especially to certain medications or foods, this phrase is vital.

41. Asking for Directions to the Hospital - 「病院はどこですか？」 **(Byouin wa doko desu ka?)**: In case you need to find a hospital, this question can guide you there.

42. Requesting Police Assistance - 「警察を呼んでください」**(Keisatsu o yonde kudasai)**: Use this phrase to ask someone to call the police.

43. Lost and Found Inquiry - 「落し物をしたかもしれません」 **(Otoshimono o shita kamoshiremasen)**: If you think you've lost something, this phrase can help you inquire about it.

44. Safety Concern - 「安全ですか？」**(Anzen desu ka?)**: To ask if a place or situation is safe, this is the phrase to use.

45. Seeking a Doctor - 「医者に会いたいです」**(Isha ni aitai desu)**: When you need to see a doctor, this phrase will express your need.

Medical Emergencies

In the unpredictable flow of life, especially when traveling in Japan, it's essential to be equipped with phrases that can aid you during medical emergencies. These phrases are designed to be straightforward and easy to understand, ensuring you can communicate effectively in critical situations.

46. Expressing a Medical Emergency - 「緊急医療が必要です」**(Kinkyuu iryou ga hitsuyou desu)**: Use this phrase to convey that you or someone else requires immediate medical attention.

47. Describing Pain - 「痛みがあります」**(Itami ga arimasu)**: To describe that you're in pain, followed by pointing to the area can help medical professionals understand your situation better.

48. Mentioning Allergies - 「アレルギー反応があります」**(Arerugii hannou ga arimasu)**: If you have allergies, especially in an emergency situation, this phrase can be critical.

49. Requesting an English-speaking Doctor - 「英語を話せる医者はいますか？」**(Eigo o hanaseru isha wa imasu ka?)**: Finding a doctor who speaks English can greatly help in understanding and explaining your medical condition.

50. Asking for a Pharmacy - 「薬局はどこですか？」**(Yakkyoku wa doko desu ka?)**: If you need to find a pharmacy to get medication, this question will be helpful.

51. Explaining Symptoms - 「熱があります」**(Netsu ga arimasu)**: To explain symptoms like fever, this simple phrase is used.

52. Indicating an Injury - 「怪我をしました」**(Kega o shimashita)**: Use this phrase to indicate that you or someone else has been injured.

53. Asking for a Hospital - 「病院に連れて行ってください」**(Byouin ni tsurete itte kudasai)**: If you need to be taken to a hospital, this phrase can express your need clearly.

54. Inquiring about Medication - 「この薬は何ですか？」**(Kono kusuri wa nan desu ka?)**: When you're given medication, it's always wise to know what it is, especially if you have specific health conditions or allergies.

55. Seeking a Dentist - 「歯医者はどこですか？」**(Haisha wa doko desu ka?)**: Dental emergencies are common, and knowing how to ask for a dentist is important.

Part 3
7. Shopping and Transactions

Directions to Hospitals and Pharmacies

When you're in a foreign country, finding your way to a hospital or pharmacy can be a daunting task, especially in an emergency. Knowing how to ask for directions in Japanese is not only practical but can be a lifesaver. This section provides phrases to help you navigate to healthcare facilities in Japan with ease.

56. Asking for the Nearest Hospital - 「一番近い病院はどこですか？」 **(Ichiban chikai byouin wa doko desu ka?)**: This phrase helps you find the closest hospital. It's straightforward and gets you the information you need quickly.

57. Inquiring About a Pharmacy - 「最寄りの薬局はどこですか？」 **(Moyori no yakkyoku wa doko desu ka?)**: Use this when you need to locate the nearest pharmacy. Pharmacies in Japan can be different from those in other countries, so this question is essential.

58. Requesting Directions - 「道を教えてください」 **(Michi o oshiete kudasai)**: This phrase is a polite way to ask for directions. It can be used in any situation where you need to find your way.

59. Confirming a Location - 「病院はこの道をまっすぐですか？」 **(Byouin wa kono michi o massugu desu ka?)**: If you're unsure whether you're heading in the right direction, this phrase can confirm your path to the hospital.

60. Seeking Help to Get There - 「病院まで案内していただけますか？」 **(Byouin made annai shite itadakemasu ka?)**: If you're struggling to find your way, this phrase asks someone to guide you to the hospital.

61. Emergency Room Location - 「救急室はどこですか？」 **(Kyuukyushitsu wa doko desu ka?)**: In an emergency, knowing how to ask for the emergency room is vital.

62. Checking Pharmacy Hours - 「薬局の営業時間は何時から何時までですか？」 **(Yakkyoku no eigyou jikan wa nanji kara nanji made desu ka?)**: It's important to know when pharmacies open and close, especially if you need medication outside regular hours.

63. Asking for Ambulance - 「救急車を呼んでください」 **(Kyuukyusha o yonde kudasai)**: If you or someone else needs immediate medical attention and can't get to a hospital, use this phrase to call an ambulance.

64. Looking for a Specific Medicine - 「この薬を探しています」 **(Kono kusuri o sagashite imasu)**: When you know the name of the medicine you need, this phrase can help you find it at the pharmacy.

65. Directions to a Specific Hospital or Clinic - 「〔病院名〕までどうやって行きますか？」 **(〔Byouin-mei〕 made dou yatte ikimasu ka?)**: If you're looking for a specific hospital or clinic, replace 〔病院名〕 with the name of the facility.

Bargaining and Prices

Shopping in Japan can be a delightful experience, filled with unique items and friendly interactions. While bargaining is not common in Japanese stores, especially in malls or chain stores, it's helpful to know some phrases that can assist you in marketplaces or independent shops where pricing might be more flexible. This section provides easy-to-use phrases for discussing prices and bargaining, ensuring a smooth shopping experience.

66. Asking the Price - 「これはいくらですか？」 **(Kore wa ikura desu ka?)**: This basic phrase is your starting point for any purchase. It's polite and direct, asking for the price of the item you're interested in.

67. Expressing Your Budget - 「私の予算は〔金額〕です」 **(Watashi no yosan wa 〔kingaku〕desu):** If you're working within a budget, this phrase lets the seller know your spending limit.

68. Asking for a Discount - 「もう少し安くできますか？」**(Mou sukoshi yasuku dekimasu ka?):** Use this phrase to inquire if the seller can lower the price. Remember, being polite increases your chances of a favorable response.

69. Checking for Sales - 「セールはいつですか？」**(Seeru wa itsu desu ka?):** This is handy for finding out when sales are happening, especially in larger stores.

70. Bargaining in a Friendly Manner - 「これを〔金額〕で買いたいです」 **(Kore o 〔kingaku〕de kaitai desu):** A soft approach to bargaining, this phrase expresses your desire to buy the item at a certain price.

71. Asking for a Better Offer - 「もっといい値段はありますか？」**(Motto ii nedan wa arimasu ka?):** If you think the item is overpriced, this phrase can prompt the seller to offer a better deal.

72. Agreeing on a Price - 「それでいいです。買います」**(Sore de ii desu. Kaimasu):** When you're happy with the price, use this phrase to confirm your purchase.

73. Declining Politely - 「考え直します。ありがとうございます」 **(Kangaenaoshimasu. Arigatou gozaimasu):** If the price is still not right for you, this phrase allows you to decline gracefully while thanking the seller.

74. Inquiring About Payment Methods - 「クレジットカードは使えますか？」**(Kurejitto kaado wa tsukaemasu ka?):** It's important to know if the shop accepts credit cards or if it's cash only.

75. Asking for a Receipt - 「レシートをもらえますか？」**(Reshiito o moraemasu ka?):** Always ask for a receipt, especially if you're buying something valuable.

Understanding these phrases will not only enhance your shopping experience but also help you navigate the retail environment in Japan with confidence. Remember, a smile and a polite demeanor go a long way in any transaction!

Sizes and Measurements

In Japan, sizes and measurements can be quite different from what you may be used to. Here are listed essential phrases to help you navigate the world of Japanese sizes, whether you're shopping for clothes, shoes, or other items. Understanding these terms will make your shopping experience more enjoyable and efficient.

76. Inquiring About Size - 「この商品のサイズは何ですか？」(Kono shouhin no saizu wa nan desu ka?): Begin by asking about the size of the item you're interested in. This basic question is a great starting point.

77. Specifying Your Size - 「私のサイズは〔サイズ〕です」(Watashi no saizu wa 〔saizu〕 desu): Let the shop assistant know your size. Remember, Japanese sizes might be different, so it's good to know your measurements in centimeters.

78. Asking for a Different Size - 「もっと大きいサイズはありますか？」(Motto ookii saizu wa arimasu ka?): If you need a larger size, this phrase will be helpful. Similarly, for a smaller size, replace 'ookii' (large) with 'chiisai' (small).

79. Trying On Clothes - 「これを試着してもいいですか？」(Kore o shichaku shite mo ii desu ka?): Use this phrase to ask if you can try on clothes. Most Japanese stores have fitting rooms.

80. Asking About Shoe Sizes - 「靴のサイズは何ですか？」(Kutsu no saizu wa nan desu ka?): If you're buying shoes, this phrase will help you find out the available sizes.

81. Inquiring About Lengths and Dimensions - 「このテーブルの長さはどれくらいですか？」(Kono teeburu no nagasa wa dore kurai desu ka?): Useful for furniture or any item where dimensions matter.

82. Confirming the Fit - 「これは私に合っていますか？」(Kore wa watashi ni atte imasu ka?): After trying something on, use this phrase to confirm if it fits well.

83. Inquiring About Customizations - 「サイズの調整は可能ですか？」(Saizu no chousei wa kanou desu ka?): If something doesn't fit, ask if it can be adjusted or altered.

84. Requesting a Different Color or Style - 「別の色（スタイル）はありますか？」 (Betsu no iro (sutairu) wa arimasu ka?): When you like the item but prefer a different color or style.

85. Checking for Stock - 「他の店舗に在庫はありますか？」 (Hoka no tenpo ni zaiko wa arimasu ka?): If your size is not available, ask if it's available at another store location.

Returns and Exchanges

Navigating the process of returns and exchanges in Japanese stores can be a bit different than what you might expect. This section of our book provides the key phrases and tips you need to handle these situations with ease and confidence.

86. Initiating a Return - 「この商品を返品したいのですが」 (Kono shouhin wo henpin shitai no desu ga): Start by expressing your desire to return an item. Remember, always be polite.

87. Explaining the Reason - 「サイズが合わないので」 (Saizu ga awanai node): If size is the issue, use this phrase. You can replace 'saizu' (size) with other reasons like 'color' (iro) or 'style' (sutairu).

88. Asking About Exchange Policy - 「交換のポリシーは何ですか？」 (Koukan no porishii wa nan desu ka?): Inquire about the store's exchange policy. Understanding the policy is crucial for a smooth process.

89. Seeking a Different Size or Color - 「違うサイズ（色）に交換してもらえますか？」 (Chigau saizu (iro) ni koukan shite moraemasu ka?): When you want to exchange an item for a different size or color.

90. Receipt Inquiry - 「レシートが必要ですか？」 (Reshiito ga hitsuyou desu ka?): Ask if you need to present a receipt for the return or exchange.

91. Time Limit for Returns - 「返品の期限はいつまでですか？」 (Henpin no kigen wa itsu made desu ka?): It's important to know the time frame in which returns or exchanges are accepted.

92. Refund Method - 「払い戻しはどのように行われますか？」 (Haraimodoshi wa dono you ni okonawaremasu ka?): Understand how refunds are processed, whether it's cash, credit, or store credit.

93. Restocking Fee Inquiry - 「返品に手数料はかかりますか？」**(Henpin ni tesuuryou wa kakarimasu ka?)**: Some stores might charge a restocking fee, so it's good to ask.

94. Non-returnable Items - 「返品不可の商品はありますか？」**(Henpin fuka no shouhin wa arimasu ka?)**: Some items might be final sale. Always check for non-returnable items.

95. Exchange Without a Receipt - 「レシートがない場合の交換は可能ですか？」**(Reshiito ga nai baai no koukan wa kanou desu ka?)**: In case you lost the receipt, ask if an exchange is still possible.

Ordering Food and Drinks

Going on a dining experience in Japan can be as delightful as it is delicious. In this section, we'll guide you through the essential phrases for ordering food and drinks, ensuring your culinary journey is as smooth and enjoyable as possible.

96. Requesting a Menu - 「メニューを見せていただけますか？」**(Menyuu o misete itadakemasu ka?)**: Always start by asking for the menu. It's your gateway to the flavors ahead.

97. Asking for Recommendations - 「おすすめは何ですか？」**(Osusume wa nan desu ka?)**: Trust the expertise of your server. They might lead you to a hidden gem on the menu.

98. Ordering a Specific Dish - 「これを一つお願いします」**(Kore o hitotsu onegaishimasu)**: When you've made your choice, use this phrase to place your order.

99. Inquiring About Ingredients - 「これには何が入っていますか？」**(Kore ni wa nani ga haitte imasu ka?)**: If you have dietary restrictions or are simply curious, don't hesitate to ask about what's in a dish.

100. Requesting a Drink - 「お水をください」**(Omizu o kudasai)**: Water is a staple. Replace 'omizu' (water) with any other drink like 'ocha' (tea) or 'biiru' (beer).

101. Asking for More Time - 「もう少し時間をください」**(Mou sukoshi jikan o kudasai)**: Need more time to decide? Use this phrase to ask for a few extra moments.

102. Special Requests - 「辛くないようにしてください」 **(Karakunai you ni shite kudasai)**: If you have specific preferences like less spice, don't be shy to communicate that.

103. Checking for Vegetarian Options - 「ベジタリアン用の料理はありますか？」 **(Bejitarian-you no ryouri wa arimasu ka?)**: Vegetarian? Make sure to check for suitable options.

104. Ordering a Set Meal - 「定食を一つください」 **(Teishoku o hitotsu kudasai)**: Set meals are a great way to enjoy a complete dining experience.

105. Asking for the Bill - 「お会計お願いします」 **(Okaikei onegaishimasu)**: When you're ready to leave, use this phrase to ask for the bill.

Dietary Restrictions

Navigating dining in Japan with dietary restrictions doesn't have to be a daunting task. With the right phrases and a bit of know-how, you can enjoy the rich culinary culture of Japan worry-free. This section is dedicated to helping you communicate your dietary needs effectively.

106. Communicating Allergies - 「アレルギーがあります」 **(Arerugī ga arimasu)**: Start by mentioning that you have allergies. Be specific about what you're allergic to, for example, 「ナッツアレルギーがあります」 (Nattsu arerugī ga arimasu) for nut allergies.

107. Gluten-Free Diet - 「グルテンフリーの食事をお願いします」 **(Gurutenfurī no shokuji o onegaishimasu)**: If you're on a gluten-free diet, this phrase will be your go-to. It clearly communicates your need for gluten-free options.

108. Vegetarian and Vegan - 「ベジタリアン用です」 **(Bejitarian-you desu)** / 「ビーガン用です」 **(Bīgan-you desu)**: Clarify your preference for vegetarian (ベジタリアン) or vegan (ビーガン) meals. It's crucial in Japan, where vegetarianism isn't as common.

109. No Pork or Beef - 「豚肉と牛肉を避けたいです」 **(Butaniku to gyūniku o saketai desu)**: If your diet excludes certain types of meat like pork or beef, use this phrase to avoid any surprises.

110. Asking for Dairy-Free - 「乳製品不使用でお願いします」 **(Nyūseihin fushiyou de onegaishimasu):** Dairy-free diets are less common in Japan, so be clear and specific about your needs.

111. No Alcohol in Food - 「料理にアルコールを使わないでください」 **(Ryōri ni arukōru o tsukawanai de kudasai):** If you wish to avoid alcohol in your food, this phrase will help you communicate that effectively.

112. Inquiring About Cooking Methods - 「この料理はどのように調理されていますか？」 **(Kono ryōri wa dono yō ni chōri sareteimasu ka?):** Understanding how a dish is prepared can help you make informed choices about what to eat.

113. Requesting Customization - 「食事の変更をお願いできますか？」 **(Shokuji no henkou o onegai dekimasu ka?):** Don't be afraid to ask for modifications to a dish to accommodate your dietary needs.

Compliments and Complaints

Eating out in Japan can be a delightful experience, and it's always helpful to know how to express your satisfaction or address issues politely. This part of the book provides phrases to communicate compliments and complaints in dining settings, ensuring you can convey your thoughts respectfully and effectively.

114. Praising the Meal - 「とても美味しいです！」 **(Totemo oishii desu!):** Use this phrase to compliment a delicious meal. Japanese chefs take great pride in their work, and a simple compliment can be very appreciated.

115. Complimenting the Chef - 「料理人の技術を褒めたいです」 **(Ryōrinin no gijutsu o hometai desu):** If you're particularly impressed, you might want to acknowledge the chef's skill. This phrase will help you express that sentiment.

116. Expressing Satisfaction - 「満足しました！」 **(Manzoku shimashita!):** After a satisfying meal, it's polite to express your contentment. It's a nice way to show gratitude for the dining experience.

117. Reporting a Problem - 「すみません、これはちょっと...」 **(Sumimasen, kore wa chotto...):** If there's an issue with your meal, start your sentence with this phrase. It's a gentle way to bring up a problem without being too direct.

118. Asking for a Replacement – 「新しいものをお願いできますか？」 **(Atarashī mono o onegaidekimasu ka?)**: If you need to request a replacement for a dish, use this phrase. It's respectful and clear.

119. Inquiring About Ingredients – 「この料理には何が入っていますか？」 **(Kono ryōri ni wa nani ga haitte imasu ka?)**: If you're curious or concerned about specific ingredients, this question can help clarify what's in your dish.

120. Requesting Adjustment – 「もう少し塩気が必要です」 **(Mō sukoshi shiokke ga hitsuyō desu)**: For minor adjustments like more salt, this phrase is appropriate. It's direct yet polite.

121. Addressing Misunderstandings – 「注文と違うものが来ました」 **(Chūmon to chigau mono ga kimashita)**: If you receive something different from what you ordered, this phrase can help rectify the situation.

Chapter 5

9. Directions and Transportation

Asking for and Giving Directions

Navigating through Japan's cities and countryside can be an adventure, and knowing how to ask for directions is key. This section provides essential phrases for asking and giving directions, ensuring you can find your way and help others too.

122. Asking for Directions - 「すみません、〇〇はどこですか？」 **(Sumimasen, 〇〇 wa doko desu ka?)**: Use this phrase when you need to find a specific place. Replace 〇〇 with your destination.

123. Understanding Basic Directions - 「左に曲がってください」 **(Hidari ni magatte kudasai)**: "Turn left," and 「右に曲がってください」 (Migi ni magatte kudasai): "Turn right," are phrases you'll often hear. Knowing these basic directions helps in following the route.

124. Inquiring About Distance - 「どのくらい遠いですか？」 **(Dono kurai tōi desu ka?)**: To know how far your destination is, this phrase will come in handy.

125. Seeking Landmarks - 「近くの目印はありますか？」 **(Chikaku no mejirushi wa arimasu ka?)**: Asking for nearby landmarks can make navigating easier.

126. Offering Directions - 「まっすぐ行って、二つ目の角を右です」 **(Massugu itte, futatsu-me no kado o migi desu)**: "Go straight and turn right at the second corner," is an example of giving simple directions.

127. Confirming the Route - 「この道をずっと行けばいいですか？」**(Kono michi o zutto ikeba ii desu ka?)**: Use this to confirm if you should continue on the same road.

128. Locating Public Transport - 「最寄りの駅はどこですか？」**(Moyori no eki wa doko desu ka?)**: To find the nearest train station, this phrase is essential.

129. Bus and Train Information - 「次のバス/電車は何時ですか？」**(Tsugi no basu/densha wa nanji desu ka?)**: If you're waiting for a bus or train, this question will help you find out when the next one arrives.

130. Seeking Assistance - 「道に迷ったようです。手伝っていただけますか？」**(Michi ni mayotta yō desu. Tetsudatte itadakemasu ka?)**: If you're lost, this polite request for help can be a lifesaver.

Public Transportation

Japan's public transportation system is a marvel of efficiency and convenience. This chapter dives into the phrases you'll need to navigate buses, trains, and more, ensuring a smooth travel experience.

131. Finding the Right Train - 「この電車は〇〇に行きますか？」**(Kono densha wa 〇〇 ni ikimasu ka?)**: Replace 〇〇 with your destination to confirm you're on the right train.

132. Buying Tickets - 「切符を一枚ください」**(Kippu o ichi-mai kudasai)**: A simple way to purchase a ticket, you can specify the number you need.

133. Seeking the Bus Stop - 「バス停はどこですか？」**(Basu-tei wa doko desu ka?)**: Essential for finding the bus stop, this question will point you in the right direction.

134. Understanding Train Schedules - 「次の電車は何時に出発しますか？」**(Tsugi no densha wa nanji ni shuppatsu shimasu ka?)**: Know when the next train departs with this query.

135. Confirming Bus Routes －「このバスは〇〇に止まりますか？」(Kono basu wa 〇〇 ni tomarimasu ka?): Replace 〇〇 with the place you want to confirm the bus stops at.

136. Locating the Subway －「地下鉄の駅はどこですか？」(Chikatetsu no eki wa doko desu ka?): Inquire about the nearest subway station with this phrase.

137. Asking for Transfers －「乗り換えはどこですか？」(Norikae wa doko desu ka?): Knowing where to transfer is crucial in Japan's complex train systems.

138. Identifying Express Trains －「これは特急ですか？」(Kore wa tokkyū desu ka?): Determine if a train is an express to avoid missing local stops.

139. Requesting a Taxi －「タクシーを呼んでください」(Takushī o yonde kudasai): Use this phrase to ask someone to call a taxi for you.

140. Inquiring About Fare －「運賃はいくらですか？」(Unchin wa ikura desu ka?): A polite way to ask about the cost of your journey, be it bus, train, or taxi.

Renting Vehicles

Exploring Japan by rental car or bike offers a unique opportunity to discover hidden gems at your own pace. This section covers the essential phrases to rent a vehicle, ensuring a hassle-free and enjoyable road adventure.

141. Finding a Rental Service －「レンタカーはどこで借りられますか？」(Rentakā wa doko de kariraremasu ka?): This question helps locate a car rental service, a crucial first step in your self-guided tour.

142. Inquiring About Rates －「料金はいくらですか？」(Ryōkin wa ikura desu ka?): Before committing, it's important to know how much the rental will cost.

143. Selecting a Vehicle －「自動車の種類を選びたいです」(Jidōsha no shurui o erabitai desu): Use this phrase when you want to choose a specific type of vehicle for your journey.

144. Discussing Insurance Options - 「保険はどうすればいいですか？」 **(Hoken wa dō sureba ii desu ka?)**: Ensuring you're covered for any unforeseen events is vital.

145. Checking Vehicle Availability - 「〇〇は利用可能ですか？」**(〇〇 wa riyō kanō desu ka?)**: Replace 〇〇 with the vehicle type you're interested in.

146. Asking for a GPS - 「**GPS**を付けてもらえますか？」**(GPS o tsukete moraemasu ka?)**: A GPS is essential for navigating unfamiliar roads.

147. Understanding Fuel Policies - 「燃料ポリシーは何ですか？」**(Nenryō porishī wa nan desu ka?)**: Knowing the fuel policy helps avoid any surprises at the end of your rental.

148. Requesting Road Assistance - 「道路のアシスタンスはありますか？」**(Dōro no ashisutansu wa arimasu ka?)**: It's reassuring to know help is available in case of any issues on the road.

149. Extending the Rental Period - 「レンタル期間を延長できますか？」**(Rentaru kikan o enchō dekimasu ka?)**: If you decide to explore further, this phrase will come in handy.

150. Returning the Vehicle - 「車をどこに返せばいいですか？」**(Kuruma o doko ni kaeseba ii desu ka?)**: Ensure a smooth return by knowing where and how to return your rental.

Chapter 6

10. Accommodation and Lodging

Hotel Check-In and Check-Out

Staying in a hotel in Japan can be a delightful experience, blending traditional hospitality with modern convenience. This section will help you navigate the check-in and check-out process smoothly with useful phrases and tips.

151. Reserving a Room - 「部屋を予約したいです」**(Heya o yoyaku shitai desu)**: Start by securing your stay. This phrase will help you book a room that suits your needs.

152. Confirming the Reservation - 「予約を確認してください」**(Yoyaku o kakunin shite kudasai)**: Upon arrival, ensure your booking is in order with this simple request.

153. Requesting Room Preferences - 「静かな部屋がいいです」**(Shizuka na heya ga ii desu)**: Whether you prefer a quiet room or one with a view, this phrase will help communicate your preference.

154. Inquiring About Amenities - 「アメニティには何が含まれていますか？」**(Ameniti ni wa nani ga fukumarete imasu ka?)**: Find out what is included in your stay, such as breakfast or Wi-Fi access.

155. Discussing Payment Methods - 「クレジットカードで支払えますか？」**(Kurejitto kādo de shiharai masu ka?)**: Clarify how you can pay for your stay.

156. Asking for a Wake-Up Call - 「起こしてもらえますか？」**(Okoshite moraemasu ka?)**: Ensure you don't miss any plans with a wake-up call.

157. Requesting Extra Services - 「追加のタオルをもらえますか？」**(Tsui ka no taoru o morae masu ka?)**: Don't hesitate to ask for extra towels or pillows to make your stay comfortable.

158. Checking Out - 「チェックアウトしたいです」**(Chekkuauto shitai desu)**: When your visit comes to an end, use this phrase to start the check-out process.

159. Discussing Late Check-Out - 「レイトチェックアウトは可能ですか？」**(Reito chekkuauto wa kanō desu ka?)**: If you need more time, ask if a late check-out is possible.

160. Providing Feedback - 「滞在はとても良かったです」**(Taizai wa totemo yokatta desu)**: Share your experience with the staff, whether it was excellent or if there were any issues.

Room Types and Amenities

When traveling in Japan, understanding the types of rooms and amenities available in accommodations can greatly enhance your experience. This section is dedicated to helping you choose the right lodging and make the most of your stay.

When selecting a room, you might encounter various types:

161. Single Room - 「シングルルーム」**(Shinguru rūmu):** Ideal for solo travelers, these rooms offer a cozy space with all the essential amenities.

162. Double Room - 「ダブルルーム」**(Daburu rūmu):** Perfect for couples, double rooms provide a comfortable bed large enough for two.

163. Twin Room - 「ツインルーム」**(Tsuin rūmu)**: Featuring two separate beds, these rooms are great for friends or colleagues traveling together.

164. Japanese-Style Room - 「和室」**(Washitsu)**: Experience traditional Japanese living with tatami flooring and futon bedding.

165. Suite - 「スイートルーム」**(Suīto rūmu)**: For those seeking luxury, suites offer spacious and often lavish accommodations.

Knowing what amenities are available is also key:

166. In-Room Wi-Fi - 「部屋のWi-Fi」(Heya no Wi-Fi): Stay connected with in-room Wi-Fi.

167. Onsen Access - 「温泉へのアクセス」(Onsen e no akusesu): Some accommodations offer access to hot spring baths, providing a unique and relaxing experience.

168. Complimentary Breakfast - 「無料の朝食」(Muryō no chōshoku): Many hotels include breakfast with your stay, ranging from Western-style buffets to traditional Japanese meals.

169. Laundry Service - 「ランドリーサービス」(Randorī sābisu): For longer stays, inquire about laundry facilities or services.

170. Room Service - 「ルームサービス」(Rūmu sābisu): Enjoy the convenience of dining in your room.

Requests and Complaints

When staying at a hotel or any lodging in Japan, it's important to know how to express your needs and concerns effectively. This chapter aims to equip you with simple phrases for making requests or lodging complaints, ensuring a comfortable stay.

Firstly, let's look at common requests you might need to make:

Extra Items: If you need an extra pillow or towel, you could say, "もう一つ枕をいただけますか？" (Mō hitotsu makura o itadakemasu ka?) meaning "Can I have one more pillow?" or "タオルをもう一つください。" (Taoru o mō hitotsu kudasai.) meaning "Please give me one more towel."

Room Adjustments: For temperature control, you might ask, "部屋の温度を調節してもらえますか？" (Heya no ondo o chōsetsu shite moraemasu ka?) meaning "Can you adjust the room temperature?"

Housekeeping Requests: To request housekeeping, say, "ルームクリーニングをお願いします。" (Rūmu kurīningu o onegaishimasu.) which translates to "I would like room cleaning, please."

Handling complaints with politeness is also essential:

Noise Issues: If the room is noisy, you could express, "隣の部屋がうるさいです。" (Tonari no heya ga urusai desu.) meaning "The next room is noisy."

Room Issues: For any room-related problems, say, "部屋に問題があります。" (Heya ni mondai ga arimasu.) which means "There is a problem with the room."

Service Concerns: In case of service issues, you might say, "サービスについて話したいです。" (Sābisu ni tsuite hanashitai desu.) meaning "I would like to talk about the service."

Chapter 7
11. Socializing and Leisure Activities

Invitations and Arrangements

In Japan, forming connections and enjoying leisure activities often involve extending and accepting invitations. This section aims to provide you with simple and useful phrases for navigating social invitations, ensuring you can partake in the vibrant social life of Japan.

Extending Invitations:

- When you want to invite someone out, you can say, "一緒にコーヒーを飲みませんか？" (Issho ni kōhī o nomimasen ka?) which translates to "Would you like to have coffee together?"
- For a more specific plan, "今度の週末に映画を見に行きませんか？" (Kondo no shūmatsu ni eiga o mi ni ikimasen ka?) means "Would you like to go see a movie this weekend?"

Responding to Invitations:

- To accept an invitation, you might say, "はい、喜んで！" (Hai, yorokonde!) which means "Yes, I'd love to!"
- If you need to decline, a polite way is, "残念ですが、その日は予定があります。" (Zannen desu ga, sono hi wa yotei ga arimasu.) translating to "Unfortunately, I have plans on that day."

Making Arrangements:

- To suggest a meeting place, "駅の前で会いましょう。" (Eki no mae de aimashō.) means "Let's meet in front of the station."
- If you need to change plans, "予定を変更しなければなりません。" (Yotei o henkō shinakereba narimasen.) translates to "I need to change the plans."

Sports and Hobbies

Exploring the world of sports and hobbies in Japan offers a fantastic way to connect with the culture and its people. Whether you're a sports enthusiast or a hobbyist, this section equips you with easy phrases to talk about your interests and engage with locals in their favorite pastimes.

Discussing Sports and Hobbies:

- To ask someone about their hobbies, you can say, "趣味は何ですか？" (Shumi wa nan desu ka?), which means "What are your hobbies?"
- If you want to share your interests, you might say, "私の趣味は写真撮影です。" (Watashi no shumi wa shashin satsuei desu.), meaning "My hobby is photography."

Joining Sports Activities:

- If you're interested in joining a sports activity, you might ask, "サッカーを一緒にしませんか？" (Sakkā o issho ni shimasen ka?), which translates to "Would you like to play soccer together?"
- To express your skill level, you can say, "私は初心者です。" (Watashi wa shoshinsha desu.), meaning "I am a beginner."

Learning New Hobbies:

- To express interest in learning a new hobby, say, "日本の茶道を習いたいです。" (Nihon no sadō o naraitai desu.), which means "I want to learn Japanese tea ceremony."

- If you are looking for recommendations, ask, "どんな趣味が面白いですか？" (Donna shumi ga omoshiroi desu ka?), meaning "What hobbies are interesting?"

Nightlife and Entertainment

Japan's nightlife and entertainment scene offers an exhilarating mix of traditional and modern experiences. Whether you're exploring the neon-lit streets of Tokyo or the quieter, historical entertainment districts in other cities, this section helps you navigate and enjoy Japan's vibrant night scene.

Exploring Entertainment Options:

- To ask about local entertainment spots, say, "ここで楽しい夜の遊び場はどこですか？" (Koko de tanoshī yoru no asobiba wa doko desu ka?), which means "Where are fun nightlife spots around here?"
- If you're interested in specific types of entertainment, you might ask, "この近くにカラオケはありますか？" (Kono chikaku ni karaoke wa arimasu ka?), meaning "Is there a karaoke place nearby?"

Experiencing Japanese Nightlife:

- For a more traditional experience, you might say, "居酒屋に行きたいです。" (Izakaya ni ikitai desu.), meaning "I want to go to an izakaya (Japanese pub)."
- To experience Japan's modern nightlife, you could ask, "人気のクラブはどこですか？" (Ninki no kurabu wa doko desu ka?), meaning "Where is a popular club?"

Joining Festivities and Events:

- If you hear about a local festival or event, ask, "その祭りに参加してもいいですか？" (Sono matsuri ni sanka shite mo ii desu ka?), meaning "Can I join in that festival?"
- For concerts or performances, inquire, "チケットはどこで買えますか？" (Chiketto wa doko de kaemasu ka?), which means "Where can I buy tickets?"

Chapter 8

12. Expressing Opinions and Feelings

Likes and Dislikes

In Japan, sharing your preferences and feelings is a key part of social interaction. This chapter is dedicated to helping you express your likes and dislikes in Japanese, an essential part of everyday conversations.

Expressing Likes:

- To say you like something, use "好きです" (Suki desu), which translates to "I like it." For example, "寿司が好きです" (Sushi ga suki desu) means "I like sushi."
- If you really enjoy something, you can emphasize it by saying "とても好きです" (Totemo suki desu), meaning "I really like it."

Sharing Dislikes:

- To express dislike, say "好きではありません" (Suki dewa arimasen), meaning "I don't like it." For instance, "辛い食べ物が好きではありません" (Karai tabemono ga suki dewa arimasen) means "I don't like spicy food."
- You can also use "嫌いです" (Kirai desu) for a stronger dislike, as in "煙草が嫌いです" (Tabako ga kirai desu), which means "I hate cigarettes."

Expressing Preferences:

- To indicate a preference, use "より好きです" (Yori suki desu), meaning "I prefer." For example, "犬より猫が好きです" (Inu yori neko ga suki desu) translates to "I prefer cats over dogs."
- For general preferences, "が好きです" (Ga suki desu) is enough, like "音楽が好きです" (Ongaku ga suki desu), meaning "I like music."

Agreement and Disagreement

Conversing in Japan often involves navigating the delicate art of agreeing and disagreeing. This section guides you through expressing agreement and disagreement in Japanese, helping you maintain harmony and respect in conversations.

Expressing Agreement:

- The most common way to agree in Japanese is saying "はい" (Hai), which simply means "Yes."
- In informal settings, you might hear "うん" (Un), which is a casual affirmation.
- To agree more strongly, use "そうですね" (Sou desu ne), translating to "That's right" or "I agree."
- For empathetic agreement, especially when someone shares their feelings or experiences, "そうですね、わかります" (Sou desu ne, wakarimasu) is used, meaning "I see, I understand."

Expressing Disagreement:

- To disagree politely, use "いいえ" (Iie), meaning "No." It's direct yet respectful.
- For a softer disagreement, "ちょっと違いますね" (Chotto chigaimasu ne) can be used, which means "It's a little different."
- In situations where you want to express a differing opinion without causing offense, "それもいいですが…" (Sore mo ii desu ga…) is helpful, translating to "That's good, but…"
- When disagreeing based on personal preference, "私は違うと思います" (Watashi wa chigau to omoimasu), meaning "I think differently," is a respectful way to express your view.

Understanding how to agree and disagree is crucial in Japanese culture, where harmony in communication is highly valued. It allows you to share your opinions and feelings while respecting the perspectives of others, fostering meaningful and respectful dialogues. Whether you're agreeing with a friend's movie choice or offering a different point of view in a discussion, these phrases will help you navigate these conversations with ease.

Expressing Emotions

In Japanese culture, sharing emotions can be subtle yet profound. This section helps you articulate your feelings in Japanese, balancing honesty with cultural sensitivity.

Happiness and Joy:

- To express happiness, use "うれしいです" (Ureshii desu), which means "I'm happy."
- For expressing joy about a specific event, "それを聞いて嬉しいです" (Sore o kiite ureshii desu), meaning "I'm glad to hear that," is appropriate.
- In casual conversations, "わあ、いいね！" (Waa, ii ne!) translates to "Wow, that's great!"

Sadness and Disappointment:

- To convey sadness, "悲しいです" (Kanashii desu) or "残念です" (Zannen desu) for disappointment are used.
- When sympathizing with someone else's misfortune, "それは残念ですね" (Sore wa zannen desu ne), meaning "That's unfortunate," is a gentle way to express empathy.

Anger and Frustration:

- Expressing anger directly is less common, but "少しイライラしています" (Sukoshi iraira shite imasu), meaning "I'm a bit irritated," is a restrained way to express frustration.
- In a more formal setting, "それには困ります" (Sore ni wa komarimasu), which means "That troubles me," can convey discontent without being too direct.

Surprise and Wonder:

- To express surprise, "びっくりしました！" (Bikkuri shimashita!) is used, meaning "I'm surprised!"
- For expressing wonder or amazement, "すごいですね！" (Sugoi desu ne!) or "驚きました" (Odorokimashita), meaning "That's amazing," are suitable.

Part 4

13. Business and Formal Interactions

Business Meetings

When engaging in business meetings in Japan, understanding the cultural nuances and language is crucial for effective communication and building relationships.

Beginning the Meeting:

- Start with a polite greeting, "おはようございます" (Ohayou gozaimasu) for good morning, or "こんにちは" (Konnichiwa) for good afternoon.
- Introduce yourself with "私の名前は [Your Name] です" (Watashi no namae wa [Your Name] desu), meaning "My name is [Your Name]."
- Use "よろしくお願いします" (Yoroshiku onegaishimasu), a versatile phrase indicating your hope for a good relationship.

Discussing Business:

- When presenting an idea, start with "提案があります" (Teian ga arimasu), meaning "I have a suggestion."
- To ask for opinions, use "ご意見を伺いたいです" (Goiken o ukagaitai desu), which means "I would like to hear your opinion."

- If you need to interject, say "失礼ですが" (Shitsurei desu ga), a polite way to interrupt, meaning "Excuse me, but..."

Agreeing and Disagreeing:

- To agree, "同意します" (Douishimasu) or simply "はい" (Hai) for yes.
- If you disagree, instead of direct opposition, try "もう少し考えてみます" (Mou sukoshi kangaete mimasu), meaning "I will consider it a bit more."

Wrapping Up:

- Summarize the meeting with "本日は貴重なご意見をありがとうございました" (Honjitsu wa kichou na goiken o arigatou gozaimashita), thanking everyone for their valuable opinions today.
- End with "またお会いできることを楽しみにしています" (Mata oai dekiru koto o tanoshimi ni shite imasu), expressing your anticipation for the next meeting.

Remember, in Japanese business culture, harmony and respect are paramount. Avoid direct confrontation and prioritize group consensus. Being aware of these subtleties will help you navigate business meetings effectively, leaving a lasting impression of professionalism and cultural sensitivity.

Formal Greetings and Introductions

Navigating the world of formal greetings and introductions in Japan requires an understanding of both language and cultural etiquette. This chapter delves into the essential phrases and customs that will help you make a positive impression in formal Japanese settings.

Initial Greeting:

- Start with a respectful bow. The depth of the bow indicates the level of respect.
- Say "はじめまして" (Hajimemashite), meaning "Nice to meet you." This phrase is used when meeting someone for the first time.

Self-Introduction:

- Introduce your name with "私の名前は [Your Name] です" (Watashi no namae wa [Your Name] desu). In formal settings, it's common to use your last name.
- Follow with your affiliation or company name: "[Company] の [Your Position] を務めています" ([Company] no [Your Position] o tsutomete imasu), meaning "I am [Your Position] at [Company]."

Exchanging Business Cards:

- Present your business card with both hands. This is a sign of respect.
- When receiving a card, take a moment to look at it carefully before putting it away.

Formal Courtesy Phrases:

- Use "どうぞよろしくお願いいたします" (Douzo yoroshiku onegaishimasu) at the end of your introduction. It conveys your hope for a good relationship.
- If you're speaking with someone of higher status, add "お世話になっております" (Osewa ni natte orimasu), meaning "Thank you for your support."

Ending the Introduction:

- Conclude with a polite "ありがとうございます" (Arigatou gozaimasu) for "Thank you."
- A closing bow signifies the end of the introduction.

Business Dining Etiquette

In Japan, business dining is not just about food; it's a crucial part of relationship-building. Understanding the etiquette can help you navigate these situations with confidence. Let's explore the key aspects:

Arrival and Seating:

- Punctuality is critical. Arriving on time, or even slightly early, is considered respectful.

- Seating order matters. Higher-ranking individuals or guests of honor typically sit farthest from the entrance. Follow the host's lead or politely ask where to sit.

Ordering and Drinking:

- Wait for the host to order. It's common for the host to choose dishes for the table, but you might be asked for preferences.
- For drinks, wait until everyone's drink is served and the host gives a toast (kanpai) before drinking.

Eating Etiquette:

- Use chopsticks correctly and never point them at others or stick them upright in a bowl of rice.
- It's polite to try a bit of everything served, even if it's unfamiliar.
- Pace yourself with the group, especially the host.

Conversation:

- Business dining is often more about socializing than discussing work. Keep conversations light and avoid controversial topics.
- Compliment the food and express gratitude for the meal and company.

Paying and Leaving:

- The host usually pays for the meal, but offering to contribute is a sign of good manners.
- Thank the host and others for the meal and company when leaving.

Remember, business dining in Japan is an art form, blending culinary enjoyment with social grace. Respecting these customs not only enhances your dining experience but also strengthens your business relationships.

Chapter 9
14. Technology and Communication

Using Phones and Internet

Navigating phone and internet usage in Japan can be a unique experience. Here's a detailed guide to help you stay connected smoothly:

Mobile Phones:

- Japan operates on a CDMA network, different from many Western countries. Ensure your phone is compatible or consider renting a Japanese phone.
- Many travelers opt for rental smartphones or SIM cards, available at airports or online.
- Public Wi-Fi can be spotty. Look for 'Free Wi-Fi' signs in cafes, train stations, and some public areas.

Internet Cafes and Manga Kissa:

- Internet cafes, known as 'Manga Kissa,' are a budget-friendly option for internet access. They also offer manga libraries, drinks, and sometimes showers.
- Rates vary, but most are reasonably priced. You can pay for a block of time, like a few hours or overnight.

Making Calls:

- For international calls, prepaid international calling cards offer good rates. These can be bought at convenience stores.
- Payphones are still somewhat common in Japan. Green and grey phones accept coins and prepaid telephone cards.

Social Media and Messaging Apps:

- Messaging apps like LINE are extremely popular in Japan. It's a handy tool for free messaging and calls.
- Social media platforms like Twitter and Instagram are also widely used for communication and sharing experiences.

Data Usage and Wi-Fi:

- If you plan to use data heavily, consider renting a pocket Wi-Fi. It offers unlimited data and can connect multiple devices.
- Many major cities have free Wi-Fi spots, but sign-up may be required, often in Japanese.

Social Media Phrases

In the fast-paced world of social media, knowing how to communicate effectively in Japanese can enrich your online interactions. This section covers key phrases and cultural nuances for engaging on social media platforms in Japan

Starting Conversations:

- "Konnichiwa, watashi no namae wa [Your Name] desu." (こんにちは、私の名前は[Your Name]です。) - "Hello, my name is [Your Name]."
- "Anata no posuto wa totemo omoshiroi desu." (あなたのポストはとても面白いです。) - "Your post is very interesting."

Commenting and Reacting:

- "Sugoi desu ne!" (すごいですね！) - "That's amazing!"
- "Kirei na shashin!" (きれいな写真！) - "Beautiful picture!"

Sharing Opinions:

- "Watashi wa [topic] ni tsuite kou omoimasu." (私は[topic]についてこう思います。) - "I think this about [topic]."
- "Anata no iken wa nani desu ka?" (あなたの意見は何ですか？) - "What is your opinion?"

Making Plans:

- "Issho ni [activity] shimasen ka?" (一緒に[activity]しませんか？) - "Shall we do [activity] together?"
- "Raishuu no [day] ni aitai desu." (来週の[day]に会いたいです。) - "I want to meet next [day]."

Expressing Appreciation:

- "Arigatou gozaimasu, anata no komento wa ureshii desu." (ありがとうございます、あなたのコメントは嬉しいです。) - "Thank you, your comment makes me happy."
- "Kono shashin o suteki to itte kurete arigatou." (この写真を素敵と言ってくれてありがとう。) - "Thank you for saying this photo is lovely."

Saying Goodbye:

- "Mata ne!" (またね！) - "See you later!"
- "Kyou wa tanoshikatta, mata kondo!" (今日は楽しかった、また今度！) - "Today was fun, until next time!"

Technological Terms

Computers and Internet:

- "Konpyuutaa" (コンピューター): The Japanese word for computer.
- "Intaanetto" (インターネット): Refers to the internet.
- "Buraunzaa" (ブラウザー): Browser, the tool used to access the internet.
- "Pasokon" (パソコン): A colloquial term for a personal computer.

- "Nettowaaku" (ネットワーク): Network, referring to internet or LAN connections.
- "Wi-Fi" (ワイファイ): Commonly used as is for wireless internet access.
- "Yuuzaa mei" (ユーザー名): Username.
- "Pasuwaado" (パスワード): Password.

Smartphones and Applications:

- "Sumaato fon" (スマートフォン): The term for smartphones.
- "Apli" (アプリ): Short for application, used for mobile apps.
- "Chuubu" (チャージ): Charge, as in charging your phone.
- "Keitai denwa" (携帯電話): Mobile phone, often shortened to "keitai."
- "Taacchi sukuriin" (タッチスクリーン): Touch screen.
- "Appu wo insutooru suru" (アップをインストールする): To install an app.

Social Media and Email:

- "SNS" (エスエヌエス): Stands for social networking service, like Facebook or Twitter.
- "Meeru" (メール): Email.
- "Akaunto" (アカウント): Account, as in a social media account.
- "Sosharu media de toukou suru" (ソーシャルメディアで投稿する): To post on social media.
- "E-meeru wo okuru" (Eメールを送る): To send an email.
- "Fairo wo tenpu suru" (ファイルを添付する): To attach a file.

Online Activities:

- "Daunroodo" (ダウンロード): Download.
- "Kensaku" (検索): Search, often used in the context of looking up information online.
- "Onrain shoppu" (オンラインショップ): Online shopping.
- "Burogu" (ブログ): Blog.
- "Sutoriimu suru" (ストリームする): To stream (videos, music, etc.).

Technical Support:

- "Tekunikaru sapooto" (テクニカルサポート): Technical support.
- "Saabaa" (サーバー): Server.
- "Koshou" (故障): Malfunction or breakdown.
- "Saabisu sentaa ni renraku suru" (サービスセンターに連絡する): To contact the service center.
- "Risetto suru" (リセットする): To reset (a device).

General Terms:

- "Puroguramu" (プログラム): Program.
- "Seikou" (正確): Accurate or correct, often used in technical contexts.
- "Puroguramingu" (プログラミング): Programming.
- "Dētabēsu" (データベース): Database.
- "Kurāudo sābisu" (クラウドサービス): Cloud services.

Chapter 10

15. Cultural and Festival Expressions

Traditional Festivals in Japan

A Celebration of Traditions and Joy

Japan's festivals are not just events; they are a vibrant testament to the nation's rich cultural tapestry. Steeped in tradition and brimming with joy, these festivals offer a window into the soul of Japan. Let's immerse ourselves in the colorful world of traditional Japanese festivals, where each celebration tells a story, each dance carries a legacy, and every cheer echoes centuries of history.

Hanami (花見): Cherry Blossom Viewing

Every spring, Japan blooms in a flurry of pink as cherry blossoms, or "sakura," adorn the streets. Hanami, the cherry blossom festival, is a time of joy and renewal. People gather under the blossoms for picnics, songs, and the simple pleasure of watching the delicate sakura petals dance in the breeze.

Gion Matsuri (祇園祭): Kyoto's Grand Festival

In July, the ancient streets of Kyoto come alive with the Gion Matsuri. Dating back over a thousand years, this festival is famous for its grand procession of floats, traditional music, and vibrant yukatas. It's a spectacle of culture, connecting the present to the historical heart of Japan.

Tanabata (七夕): The Star Festival

Tanabata, celebrated in July or August, is a festival of star-crossed love. Inspired by a Chinese legend, it's a day when people write their wishes on colorful paper strips and hang them on bamboo trees, hoping the stars will grant their desires.

Obon (お盆): Honoring Ancestral Spirits

In August, Obon is observed to honor the spirits of ancestors. It's a time for family reunions, visiting ancestral graves, and the famous Bon Odori dance. Lanterns light up the night, symbolizing the spirits' journey back to the afterlife.

Kanda Matsuri (神田祭): Tokyo's Dynamic Celebration

Alternating with Sanno Matsuri every other year, Kanda Matsuri is one of Tokyo's three major festivals. It features a massive parade with hundreds of participants, portable shrines, and a lively atmosphere, showcasing Tokyo's energy and spirit.

Awa Odori (阿波踊り): The Dance of Fools

During the Obon season, Tokushima city hosts Awa Odori, one of Japan's largest dance festivals. Thousands dance through the streets in a mesmerizing display, accompanied by traditional instruments, chanting the phrase, "Fools dance, and fools watch; if both are fools, you might as well dance!"

Sapporo Snow Festival (札幌雪まつり): Winter's Wonderland

In February, Sapporo transforms into a winter wonderland during the Sapporo Snow Festival. Gigantic snow sculptures, ice art, and twinkling lights turn the city into a magical spectacle, drawing visitors from around the world.

These festivals are not just dates on the calendar; they are living stories woven into the fabric of Japanese life. They celebrate nature's beauty, honor the past, and continue a legacy of joy and community. For travelers, participating in these festivals offers a taste of Japan's heart and soul—a journey through time and tradition that remains unforgettable.

Cultural Landmarks in Japan

Discovering Japan's Historical Wonders

Going on a journey through Japan's cultural landmarks is like traveling through time. Each site, with its unique history and beauty, tells a story of Japan's past and present. These landmarks are not just stone and wood; they are living narratives of history, art, and tradition. Let's explore some of Japan's most iconic cultural landmarks, where every corner whispers tales of yore and every path leads to a discovery.

Fushimi Inari Taisha (伏見稲荷大社)

In Kyoto, this Shinto shrine is famous for its thousands of vermilion torii gates, which create a path up the mountain. It's a place of wonder, where each gate represents a wish or a thank you from visitors and locals alike.

Himeji Castle (姫路城)

Also known as 'White Heron Castle' for its elegant white appearance, Himeji Castle is a masterpiece of wooden architecture and a symbol of Japan's feudal history. Its complex design and preserved structure make it a must-visit for history enthusiasts.

Kinkaku-ji (金閣寺): The Golden Pavilion

This Zen Buddhist temple in Kyoto, covered in gold leaf, shimmers beside a tranquil pond, creating a scene of breathtaking beauty. It's a perfect representation of harmony between architecture and nature.

Itsukushima Shrine (厳島神社)

Located on Miyajima Island, this shrine is famous for its floating torii gate. At high tide, the gate and shrine seem to float on water, offering a magical and serene view, especially at sunset.

Nikko's Toshogu Shrine (日光東照宮)

Nestled in the mountains of Nikko, this lavishly decorated shrine is the final resting place of Tokugawa Ieyasu, the founder of the Tokugawa shogunate. Its intricate carvings, including the famous 'See no Evil, Hear no Evil, Speak no Evil' monkeys, are a spectacle of craftsmanship.

Todai-ji Temple (東大寺) in Nara

Home to the Great Buddha, this temple's Daibutsuden (Great Buddha Hall) is one of the largest wooden structures in the world. The immense bronze Buddha statue within is a testament to the spiritual and artistic heritage of Japan.

Matsumoto Castle (松本城)

Known for its striking black exterior and moon-viewing turret, Matsumoto Castle offers a glimpse into the samurai era. Its wooden interiors and strategic defense design are as fascinating as its history.

The Peace Memorial Park in Hiroshima (広島平和記念公園)

A symbol of peace and resilience, this park and its museum recount the tragic history of the atomic bombing. The iconic A-Bomb Dome stands as a haunting reminder and a hope for world peace.

Senso-ji Temple (浅草寺)

In Tokyo's Asakusa district, Senso-ji is an ancient Buddhist temple known for its vibrant red gates and the bustling Nakamise shopping street. The temple is alive with history and the energy of visitors and locals, making it a must-see spot.

Mount Fuji (富士山)

Japan's iconic, snow-capped mountain is not just a natural wonder but a cultural symbol too. Whether you're admiring it from a distance or climbing its slopes, Mount Fuji is a sight of awe and inspiration.

Shirakawa-go and Gokayama Villages (白川郷・五箇山)

These villages, with their traditional gassho-zukuri thatched houses, look like they're straight out of a fairy tale. Visiting here is like stepping back in time to a peaceful, rural Japan.

Kenrokuen Garden in Kanazawa (兼六園)

This beautiful garden, known for its perfect landscape design, represents the best of traditional Japanese gardening. It's a place of tranquility where nature's beauty is on full display in every season.

The Bamboo Forest of Arashiyama (嵐山の竹林)

Near Kyoto, this bamboo grove is a magical place. Walking through the towering green bamboo is like entering another world, both mystical and calming.

Okinawa's Shuri Castle (首里城)

A symbol of the Ryukyu Kingdom's rich history, Shuri Castle stands out with its unique architectural style. It's a colorful testament to Okinawa's distinct cultural heritage.

Akihabara District (秋葉原)

Known as the 'Electric Town' in Tokyo, Akihabara is a buzzing hub for electronics, manga, anime, and all things modern Japanese pop culture. It's a vibrant, energetic place that shows a different side of Japan's cultural landscape.

The Historic Villages of Kiso Valley (木曽谷の歴史的村落)

Walking through the post towns of Tsumago and Magome in the Kiso Valley is like walking through a living museum. The well-preserved Edo-period buildings and the scenic mountain paths make for a memorable experience.

Understanding Japanese Historical and Religious Terms

Shogun (将軍)

Once the military rulers of Japan, shoguns held immense power. Their era was marked by warrior code, castles, and epic battles, shaping much of Japan's history.

Samurai (侍)

The famed warriors of Japan, samurai were known for their strict code of honor, bravery, and skills in martial arts. They were the protectors and enforcers of their time.

Kabuki (歌舞伎)

A traditional Japanese drama known for its elaborate costumes and expressive performances. Kabuki is a window into Japan's cultural storytelling and art.

Geisha (芸者)

Geisha are skilled performers and hostesses in Japanese culture. They are trained in various arts like classical music, dance, and conversation.

Zen (禅)

A school of Buddhism that emphasizes meditation and intuition. Zen gardens and temples reflect this serene, minimalist philosophy.

Shinto (神道)

Japan's indigenous faith focuses on kami (spirits) and rituals that connect people with nature and ancestors. Shrines across Japan are places of Shinto worship.

Kimonos (着物)

Traditional Japanese clothing known for its beauty and elegance. Kimonos are not just garments; they are artistic expressions of Japanese culture.

Haiku (俳句)

A form of short poetry that captures the essence of a moment or emotion in just a few words. Haiku is a beloved and enduring art form in Japan.

Tea Ceremony (茶道)

More than making tea, it's a ceremonial way of preparing and presenting matcha (green tea). It's about aesthetics, harmony, and mindfulness.

Origami (折り紙)

The art of paper folding. Origami is not just a craft; it's a symbol of creativity and peace, often used in various cultural and religious ceremonies.

Katana (刀)

The katana is more than a sword; it's a symbol of the samurai spirit. Crafted with great skill, it represents the warrior's strength and honor in Japanese history.

Kaiseki (懐石)

A traditional multi-course Japanese meal. Kaiseki is a culinary art form that balances taste, texture, and presentation, deeply rooted in Zen philosophy.

Torii Gate (鳥居)

The iconic red gates at the entrance of Shinto shrines. They mark the transition from the mundane to the sacred, symbolizing a passage to a place closer to the kami.

Noh Theater (能)

A classical Japanese performance art, combining drama, music, and dance. Noh plays often explore themes like history, spirituality, and the supernatural.

Kabuto (兜)

The traditional helmet worn by samurai. It's not just protective gear; it's a work of art, often adorned with intricate designs symbolizing power and valor.

Bonsai (盆栽)

The art of growing miniature trees. Bonsai reflects the Japanese aesthetic of wabi-sabi, finding beauty in imperfection and transience.

Sakura (桜)

Cherry blossoms, a quintessential symbol of Japan. They represent the beauty and fragility of life, celebrated during hanami (flower viewing) festivals.

Ryokan (旅館)

Traditional Japanese inns that offer a glimpse into Japan's hospitality and lifestyle, often featuring tatami floors, futons, and communal baths.

Ikebana (生け花)

The Japanese art of flower arrangement. More than just decoration, ikebana is a disciplined art form that symbolizes harmony, respect, and purity.

Sumo (相撲)

Japn's national sport, sumo wrestling is steeped in Shinto ritual. The sport is more than a physical contest; it's a performance that honors spiritual traditions.

Onsen (温泉)

Natural hot springs and the bathing facilities around them. Onsen are not just places for relaxation but also hold cultural significance in purification rituals.

Tatami (畳)

Traditional Japanese straw mats used as flooring. Their size and use in rooms follow specific rules, reflecting the Japanese preference for order and simplicity.

Understanding these terms is like opening doors to different eras and aspects of Japanese culture. They reveal the layers of history, values, and traditions that make Japan uniquely captivating. Each term is a thread in the fabric of Japan's rich cultural tapestry, inviting you to explore and appreciate the depth and beauty of its heritage. Whether it's the disciplined life of a samurai, the tranquil world of Zen, or the vibrant spectacle of Kabuki, these historical and religious terms offer a fascinating glimpse into the soul of Japan.

Part 5

16. Tips for Effective Communication in Japan

Understanding Body Language and Non-Verbal Cues in Japan

Communicating effectively in Japan goes beyond just mastering the language; it involves understanding the dance of non-verbal cues and body language. Let's delve into this intriguing aspect of Japanese culture.

In Japan, bowing, known as 'Ojigi', is an art form in itself. More than just a way of saying hello or goodbye, the depth and duration of a bow speak volumes about respect, gratitude, and even apology. It's a silent yet powerful way of expressing feelings without words.

Eye contact in Japan treads a fine line. Unlike in some cultures where direct eye contact is a sign of confidence, in Japan, it's a balancing act. A little eye contact is good; too much can be seen as a challenge or a sign of disrespect, especially in formal situations.

When it comes to facial expressions, don't expect emotions to be worn on the sleeve. A smile in Japan can be a Swiss Army knife, used not just for happiness but also for discomfort, apology, or to mask true feelings.

Silence, often uncomfortable in the West, is golden in Japan. It's a sign of agreement, reflection, or respect. In a conversation, silence is a participant, giving space and weight to words spoken and unspoken.

Personal space is sacred in Japan. Respecting this invisible bubble, especially when talking, shows understanding and respect for personal boundaries, a cornerstone of Japanese social interaction.

In terms of physical gestures, you'll find fewer grand gestures and more subtle movements. For instance, a simple hand wave in front of the face is a common way to say 'no' or to deny something gently.

Nodding in Japan is akin to saying, "I'm listening, I understand," more than "I agree." It's a sign of engagement in the conversation, not necessarily endorsement of the words.

Posture is paramount. Good posture shows respect and attentiveness, while slouching or leaning too casually can come across as disinterest or disrespect.

Japanese culture appreciates subtlety, and this is evident in how surprise is expressed. A small gasp or a hand covering the mouth, especially among women, is a common and modest way to show surprise.

Physical contact, like hugging or back-patting, common in the West, is rare in Japan, especially in formal contexts. A handshake, though adopted from the West, is softer and quicker.

In expressing gratitude, a small bow combined with a soft 'thank you' or 'Arigatou' is customary. It shows appreciation in a humble and respectful manner.

In Japan, the unsaid, the subtle, and the implicit carry as much, if not more, weight than the spoken word. It's a dance of gestures, expressions, and silences that, when understood, can lead to deeper connections and a more profound understanding of Japanese culture and its people.

Avoiding Misunderstandings in Japan

Navigating the waters of communication in Japan can be like a gentle dance. Knowing how to avoid misunderstandings is key to ensuring smooth interactions, whether you're on a business trip, a cultural exploration, or just enjoying the beauty of Japan.

Firstly, being aware of the subtlety of Japanese language is important. Directness is often avoided in favor of more indirect expressions. For instance, a 'no' might often be conveyed through phrases like 'it's a bit difficult' or 'I'll consider it.' Understanding these nuances helps in deciphering the true meaning behind words.

Humility is woven into the fabric of Japanese communication. Overconfidence or self-promotion can sometimes be perceived as arrogance. It's often better to understate achievements and let actions speak for themselves.

Silence is a critical component of conversation in Japan. It's not merely a pause but a space for reflection and respect. Embrace these moments of quietude; they're not awkward silences but a part of the conversational rhythm.

Remember, 'yes' can mean different things. A nod or a 'hai' (yes) in Japan often means 'I hear you' rather than 'I agree.' This distinction is vital to understand, especially in a business setting where agreement and understanding can be poles apart.

Being attentive to non-verbal cues is as important as listening to words. A slight bow, a respectful nod, or a soft smile can convey much more than spoken language. These gestures are the unspoken poetry of Japanese culture.

In Japan, the context is everything. The setting, the relationship between speakers, and the occasion all influence how messages are conveyed and interpreted. For example, what's appropriate in a casual setting with friends might not be in a formal business meeting.

It's also crucial to pay attention to what is not said. In Japan, being overtly explicit is not the norm. Reading between the lines, understanding the situation, and observing the atmosphere, or 'kuuki wo yomu', is an art in itself.

Lastly, politeness is paramount. Using polite language, especially when addressing someone in a higher position or older than you, is a sign of respect. Learning basic polite phrases in Japanese goes a long way in showing respect and avoiding misunderstandings.

By being mindful of these aspects, your journey through the beautiful and complex landscape of Japanese communication will not only be enriching but also free from the pitfalls of misunderstandings. It opens the door to a deeper understanding and appreciation of the rich tapestry of Japanese culture and its people.

Adapting to Regional Accents in Japan

Imagine you're in Tokyo, where the language sounds neat and standard, like a well-tied obi on a kimono. It's the kind of Japanese often heard on TV. But as you journey to Osaka, the language takes a playful turn. Words are stretched a bit longer, like a friendly smile, and sentences end with a warm, sing-song intonation. It's like listening to a cheerful tune.

Then, there's the Kyoto dialect, elegant and polite, reflecting the city's ancient heritage. Here, the language flows smoothly, like the calm waters of the Kamo River. It's more formal, with a gentle touch, like the soft rustle of silk kimonos.

In the northern region of Hokkaido, the language becomes straightforward, like the clear, crisp air of the region. And down in Okinawa, the accent sings of the islands' tropical breeze, with a melody that's quite different from mainland Japan.

Now, adapting to these accents doesn't mean you have to master each one. It's more about tuning your ear to the rhythm and melody of the language. Just like enjoying different genres of music, appreciate the unique flavor each dialect brings. It makes the conversation more colorful and the experience richer.

When you're trying to communicate, it's okay to stick to standard Japanese. Most people across Japan understand it. But showing interest in their local dialect can be a lovely way to connect. It's like saying, "I appreciate where you're from."

Tokyo - Standard Japanese (標準語, Hyōjungo)

- **Characteristics**: Clear, crisp pronunciation with no accentuation on syllables. It's the most widely understood and used dialect in Japan.
- **Useful Approach**: Focus on learning standard Japanese. It serves as a universal key for communication across the country.

Kansai Region - Kansai-ben (関西弁)

- **Osaka** Dialect: Known for its friendly and expressive nature. Phrases end with "-hen" instead of "-nai" for negatives, like "shiranai" becomes "shirahen."

- **Kyoto** Dialect: Polite and refined, reflecting the city's historical elegance. For example, "arigatō" (thank you) is often pronounced more softly and elongated.
- **Tips**: Watch local TV shows or comedies from the Kansai region. It's a fun way to get accustomed to the dialect's intonation and expressions.
- **Hiroshima - Hiroshima-ben (広島弁)**
- **Characteristics**: It has a unique intonation and uses distinct words, like "ja" instead of "deshou" for speculation.
- **Adapting Tip**: Listen to local conversations, especially in traditional settings like markets. It helps in picking up the dialect's rhythm.
- **Tohoku Region - Tohoku-ben (東北弁)**
- **Features**: Known for its strong and distinctive accent with elongated vowels.
- **Challenge**: It can be difficult to understand due to its unique intonation and vocabulary.
- **Strategy**: Practice patience and don't hesitate to ask for clarification or repetition. Engage with local media for better acclimatization.
- **Okinawa - Uchinaaguchi (沖縄口)**
- **Distinctiveness**: More than a dialect, it's a separate language with unique words and phrases.
- **Approach**: Learn some basic Okinawan phrases as a sign of respect and interest in the local culture.

Practical Tips for Adaptation:

- **Active Listening**: Pay close attention to how locals speak, noting intonation, speed, and unique phrases.
- **Practice Speaking**: Try mimicking the accent in a respectful way. It shows your effort to integrate and respect their culture.
- **Local Media Consumption**: Watch regional TV programs, listen to local radio, and engage with regional music. It helps in familiarizing yourself with the local way of speaking.
- **Cultural Immersion**: Participate in local events and interact with natives. Immersing yourself in the culture makes understanding accents easier.
- **Language Exchange**: Engage with locals who want to learn English. This mutual exchange can be a great way to learn regional nuances.

- **Patience and Openness**: Be patient with yourself. Understanding accents takes time. Stay open and curious

Chapter 11

17. Cultural Notes and Taboos

Understanding Japanese Etiquette

In the heart of Japan lies a world of etiquette, a place where manners and customs shape daily interactions. Understanding these cultural nuances is key to forming respectful and meaningful connections in Japan.

The Art of Bowing

Bowing in Japan is not just a gesture; it's a language of respect. Whether greeting someone, expressing thanks, or apologizing, the depth and duration of your bow convey your sincerity. It's a dance of humility, where a deeper, longer bow often means greater respect or seriousness.

The Subtlety of Gift-Giving

Gift-giving in Japan is a thoughtful process, full of symbolism. Presents are often wrapped meticulously, and it's customary to give and receive gifts with both hands. The act itself is more about showing appreciation and maintaining relationships than the gift.

The Quiet of Public Spaces

In Japan, public spaces like trains and buses are zones of quietude. Talking loudly on your phone or in groups is considered disruptive. This respect for communal peace extends to many aspects of Japanese life, where harmony and consideration for others are deeply ingrained.

The Ritual of Eating

Mealtime in Japan is a ritual in itself. It starts with the phrase "itadakimasu" (I gratefully receive) and ends with "gochisousama" (thank you for the meal). Remember, slurping noodles is acceptable, even appreciated, as it shows you're enjoying the meal. However, sticking chopsticks vertically in rice is a taboo, as it resembles a funeral ritual.

The Respect for Nature

Japan's deep respect for nature influences its culture profoundly. Whether it's appreciating the fleeting beauty of cherry blossoms or the changing autumn leaves, this connection with nature is a crucial part of Japanese life. It teaches the beauty of the moment and respect for the environment.

The Importance of Cleanliness

Cleanliness in Japan goes beyond personal hygiene; it's a reflection of one's respect for themselves and others. The practice of taking off shoes before entering someone's home symbolizes leaving the dirt and chaos of the outside world behind. This extends to public spaces too, where cleanliness is maintained religiously.

The Unspoken Rules

Much of Japanese etiquette is unspoken, learned through observation and experience. For example, waiting in line patiently, not pointing with your finger, and using polite language when speaking, especially to elders or in formal situations, are all integral parts of Japanese etiquette.

Navigating Social Situations in Japan

When you step into the social landscape of Japan, you enter a world where subtlety and respect are the pillars of interaction. Understanding how to navigate these social situations can enhance your experience and help you form deeper connections.

The Harmony of Group Dynamics

In Japan, the group often takes precedence over the individual. It's common for people to think about the well-being of the group before expressing personal desires. This means in social gatherings, decisions may lean towards what benefits the group as a whole rather than individual preferences.

Reading the Air (Kuuki wo Yomu)

'Kuuki wo yomu' literally means 'reading the air'. It's an essential skill in Japanese social interactions. It involves understanding unspoken cues and the mood of the situation to respond appropriately. It's about sensing what others feel or think without direct communication.

The Subtle Art of Refusal

Saying 'no' directly is often avoided in Japanese culture. Instead, ambiguous phrases or indirect language are used. For example, if someone says 'it's a bit difficult', it often means 'no'. Learning to understand and use these subtleties can prevent misunderstandings.

The Value of Apologies

Apologies in Japan are not just expressions of regret; they're a way to maintain harmony and show respect. Even if you're not directly at fault, offering an apology for any inconvenience caused is a common practice. It shows your awareness of and sensitivity to the feelings of others.

Expressing Gratitude

Gratitude is a deeply rooted value. Simple phrases like 'arigatou gozaimasu' (thank you) are powerful. They acknowledge the effort of others and are essential in everyday interactions, from receiving a service to being helped with directions.

The Role of Silence

Silence in a conversation is not necessarily awkward or negative. It's often seen as a thoughtful pause, a moment to process and respect what's been said. Embracing these moments can lead to more meaningful conversations.

Understanding Non-Verbal Cues

Non-verbal communication is crucial. A slight bow, a smile, or the way someone hands over a business card—these actions speak volumes. Observing and mirroring these subtle gestures can help in forming a respectful interaction.

The Importance of Context

In Japan, the context in which a social interaction occurs can significantly influence the behavior and expectations. For instance, the way one behaves in a formal business meeting versus a casual gathering with friends can be starkly different. Understanding the context helps you choose the appropriate tone, language, and behavior.

Respect for Elders and Hierarchy

Japanese culture places a strong emphasis on respecting elders and observing hierarchical relationships. This respect is often shown through language, gestures, and seating arrangements. For example, in a group setting, it's customary for the eldest or most senior person to lead the conversation, and others show their respect by listening attentively.

Gift-Giving Etiquette

Gift-giving is a common practice in Japan and is laden with meaning. It is essential to give and receive gifts with both hands as a sign of respect. Also, the presentation of the gift matters as much as the gift itself; thus, careful wrapping is crucial. When receiving a gift, it's polite to resist a bit before accepting, showing that you're not greedy.

The Role of Humility

Humility is a valued trait. It's common to downplay one's achievements or deflect compliments. For instance, if someone praises your work or a skill, a typical response might be 'I still have a lot to learn' instead of directly accepting the compliment. This humility helps maintain group harmony and prevents the appearance of arrogance.

Expressing Agreement and Disagreement

Agreeing or disagreeing in a Japanese social context is often less about the content of the conversation and more about maintaining harmony. Direct disagreement is rare and can be considered confrontational. Instead, people might express disagreement subtly, using phrases like "That might be difficult" or "I will think about it," which implies a polite no.

Attending Social Gatherings

When attending social gatherings, punctuality is key. Being on time, or even slightly early, is seen as a sign of respect. In many social settings, especially meals, it is common to wait for the senior person to start eating or drinking before others follow suit.

Understanding Implicit Communication

A significant part of Japanese communication is implicit. It relies on an understanding of the context, non-verbal cues, and the shared unspoken understanding between people. This can be challenging for outsiders, but paying attention to the subtleties in conversation and behavior can provide valuable clues.

Sensitivity to Non-Verbal Reactions

Paying attention to non-verbal reactions is crucial. A slight change in facial expression, tone of voice, or even a pause can indicate comfort or discomfort. Adapting your behavior based on these cues is essential to maintain the comfort and harmony of the group.

Cultural Dos and Don'ts in Japan

When you're in Japan, knowing what to do and what not to do makes a big difference. It's not just about manners; it's about showing respect and understanding their way of life. Here are some important cultural dos and don'ts:

1. Respect Personal Space:

In Japan, personal space is important. Even in crowded places, try not to bump into others or invade their personal space. It's seen as respectful to maintain a polite distance.

2. Be Mindful of Your Shoes:

In many places, like someone's home or certain traditional restaurants, you need to take off your shoes. There are usually slippers for you to wear inside. Wearing shoes indoors is a big no-no.

3. Proper Greetings are Key:

A bow is a common way to greet in Japan. The depth of the bow shows how much respect you have for the other person. A slight nod is casual and friendly.

4. Handling Money:

Don't hand money directly to cashiers. Instead, use the small tray provided at the counter. This is more polite and is the usual way of handling transactions.

5. Eating Etiquette:

If you're eating noodles like ramen, it's okay to slurp. It shows you're enjoying the meal. But, don't stick your chopsticks upright in a bowl of rice, as it resembles a funeral ritual.

6. Quiet in Public Places:

Japanese people value a quiet and peaceful environment. Talking loudly, especially in public transport, is frowned upon. It's about being considerate to those around you.

7. Recycling and Trash:

Japan takes recycling seriously. Be sure to follow the rules for separating trash. It's not just being neat; it's showing you care for the environment.

8. Photography with Respect:

Always ask before taking photos of people or in shops. It's about respecting privacy and boundaries.

9. Queueing:

Whether it's waiting for the train or buying food, queueing is orderly in Japan. Cutting in line is considered very rude.

10. Gift Giving:

If you're visiting someone, a small gift is a nice gesture. It doesn't have to be expensive, but wrapping it nicely is appreciated.

11. Respect the Queue for Trains:

In Japan, people form neat lines to board trains. It's important to wait for passengers to disembark before getting on. Rushing or pushing is considered very impolite.

12. Sensitivity to Smoking Rules:

Smoking in public places is generally restricted in Japan. Look for designated smoking areas. Ignoring these rules can be seen as disrespectful.

13. Handling of Business Cards:

If you're in a professional setting, treat business cards with respect. Use both hands to receive and give them, and take a moment to look at the card before putting it away.

14. Silence Your Phone in Public:

In public transports like trains and buses, it's polite to keep your phone on silent mode. Talking on the phone is generally frowned upon in these settings.

15. Be Cautious with Physical Contact:

Public displays of affection, like hugging or kissing, are less common in Japan. It's better to err on the side of caution and avoid making others uncomfortable.

16. Conservative Dressing:

Japanese culture tends to be conservative when it comes to dress code. Avoid overly casual attire in professional or formal settings.

17. Tipping is Not Customary:

In Japan, tipping is not a common practice. In fact, it can sometimes be seen as rude or embarrassing. The service culture in Japan is about pride in one's work, so a polite thank you is more appreciated.

18. Respect Sacred Sites:

When visiting shrines or temples, be respectful. There are often specific rituals or customs, like washing your hands at the entrance. It's best to observe and follow the local customs.

19. Don't Point with Your Chopsticks:

During a meal, avoid using your chopsticks to point at something or someone. It's considered impolite. Also, don't pass food directly from your chopsticks to someone else's, as this resembles a funeral ritual.

20. Be Wary of 'Yes' and 'No':

In Japanese culture, direct refusals or negative responses are often avoided. A 'yes' might sometimes mean 'I understand' rather than agreement. Pay attention to non-verbal cues to get a better sense of what is being communicated.

Chapter 12

18. Regional Variations in Language

Dialects and Accents

Japan is a land with a rich tapestry of dialects and accents, each adding its unique flavor to the language. As a traveler, understanding these regional differences can be both fascinating and crucial for smooth communication.

Tokyo Dialect (Standard Japanese):

Tokyo's dialect, often considered standard Japanese, is what you'll hear in most textbooks and media. It's the most widely understood across Japan, making it a safe choice for beginners.

Osaka/Kansai Dialect:

Dive into the Kansai region, and you'll encounter a dialect that's both playful and expressive. Known for its distinctive intonation, the Kansai dialect infuses conversations with a sense of humor and warmth. Phrases like "ookini" for thank you are a hallmark of this dialect.

Hokkaido Dialect:

Travel north to Hokkaido, and you'll notice a dialect influenced by the region's history and climate. It's known for its straightforwardness and clarity, reflecting the open nature of Hokkaido's landscapes.

Okinawa Dialect:

Heading far south to Okinawa, you'll experience a dialect that's almost a language of its own. With its roots in the Ryukyuan languages, it represents the unique cultural heritage of the islands.

Kyushu Dialect:

Kyushu's dialects, with their distinctive tonal variations, can be intriguing. They often sound softer and more melodious, reflecting the serene nature of the region.

Tohoku Dialect:

The dialects of Tohoku, in the northeast, are known for their strong accent and unique vocabulary. They may seem challenging to understand at first, but they embody the resilient spirit of the region.

Understanding and Adapting:

While learning all these dialects isn't necessary, being aware of them enhances your understanding of Japanese culture. You can appreciate the nuances in conversations and connect more deeply with locals. It's like unlocking different levels of a game, each level offering new sounds, expressions, and cultural insights.

As you travel through Japan, try listening to the local dialects, and maybe even learn a phrase or two. It's a sign of respect and interest in the local culture, and it can open doors to heartfelt interactions and experiences.

Understanding Regional Slang and Idioms

When you travel across Japan, you'll notice something fun about the way people talk. Every place has its own special words and phrases, like a secret language that tells you so much about the area and its people. Let's explore some of these cool local words and what they really mean.

In Tokyo and Nearby Places:

People in and around Tokyo often use trendy words that you might hear in TV shows or read in manga. One such word is "マジで？ " (maji de?), which is a way of saying "Really?" It's like when you hear something so surprising or hard to believe, you just have to ask if it's true. It shows how fast things change in Tokyo and how people there always keep up with the latest stuff.

Osaka, Kyoto, and Kobe:

Now, head over to places like Osaka, and you'll hear people using words that are more playful. For example, "なんでやねん!" (nande yanen!) is a phrase you'll often hear. It's a fun way to show you're surprised or can't believe what you just heard. It's like saying "No way!" or "You're kidding!" in English. People in this area are known for being friendly and loving a good laugh, and their way of speaking really shows that.

Down in Kyushu:

In Kyushu, folks use words that are straight to the point. "ばってん" (batten) means "but" or "however." It's like when you're talking and you want to add something more or take a turn in the conversation. It's a simple word, but it tells you that people there like to speak their minds clearly.

Up in Tohoku:

In the Tohoku region, there's a word "だべ" (dabe), which is a bit like saying "I guess" or "maybe." It's used when people aren't too sure about something or when they're thinking aloud. It gives you a hint that people in Tohoku might be a bit more thoughtful or reserved when they talk.

Okinawa's Unique Words:

Okinawa is really special because it has its own history and traditions. Here, you'll hear "めんそーれ" (mensoore), a word that's all about welcoming someone. It's like saying "come on in" or "welcome!" This word is perfect for Okinawa because people there are super friendly and always happy to meet new friends.

Hokkaido's Practical Words:

Last stop, Hokkaido! It's pretty cold and wild up there, so people use words that are practical. "しゃあない" (shaanai) means "it can't be helped" or "oh well." It's used when something didn't go as planned, but you're okay with it and ready to move on. It shows that people in Hokkaido are tough and don't get too worried about small problems.

Embracing Local Customs and Phrases

Traveling through Japan, you get to see that every place has its own unique way of speaking. It's like each city or town has its own special flavor of language. Let's dive into how local customs shape the phrases you'll hear, making every conversation a new adventure.

Tokyo's Energetic Expressions:

In the bustling streets of Tokyo, you'll hear phrases that buzz with the city's energy. People might say "ヤバイ!" (yabai!) when they're amazed or surprised. This word captures the fast-paced, exciting vibe of Tokyo.

Osaka's Friendly Banter:

Down in Osaka, people love to chat and joke around. You'll often hear "おおきに" (ookini), which means "thank you" in their dialect. It's a warm, friendly phrase that shows Osaka's cheerful spirit.

Kyoto's Polite Speech:

Kyoto, with its ancient temples and traditions, has a more formal and polite way of speaking. You might hear "おてすうをかけます" (otesuu wo kakemasu), which is a respectful way to say "I will take care of it." It reflects the city's elegant and courteous culture.

Hokkaido's Straightforward Style:

In the cooler climate of Hokkaido, people are known for being straightforward and honest. "どうだい？ " (doudai?), meaning "How is it?" or "What do you think?", is a common phrase that gets right to the point.

Okinawa's Relaxed Language:

In the tropical paradise of Okinawa, the language is as relaxed as the ocean breeze. "ちゅーがなびら" (chuuganabira), meaning "take it easy" or "no rush," is a phrase that captures the laid-back island lifestyle.

Tohoku's Thoughtful Words:

The Tohoku region, known for its beautiful landscapes, has a language that reflects its serene nature. "けっこうだべ" (kekko dabe), which means "that's fine" or "that's good," shows a sense of contentment and appreciation for the simple things in life.

Afterword

As we bring our journey through the "Easy Japanese Phrase Book" to a close, let's take a moment to reflect on the vibrant tapestry of culture, language, and experiences that make Japan truly unique. From the neon-lit streets of Tokyo to the tranquil gardens of Kyoto, each page of this book has been a step into the rich and diverse world of Japan.

Stories and Laughs Along the Way

Remember the time you tried ordering ramen in Tokyo using the phrase "おいしいラーメンをください" (oishii ramen wo kudasai), and ended up in a delightful conversation with a local chef? Or that hilarious moment in Osaka when you accidentally mixed up "かわいい" (kawaii, cute) with "こわい" (kowai, scary), describing a fluffy kitten? These are the moments that bring this book to life, turning language learning into a joyful adventure.

Japan's Endless Discoveries

Japan is a land of endless discoveries, and this book is your key to unlocking them. Whether it's navigating bustling city streets, partaking in serene tea ceremonies, or exploring historical landmarks, every phrase you've learned opens a door to deeper understanding and connection.

Looking Forward

As you continue to explore Japan, this book will be more than just a guide; it will be a companion that grows with you. Each return visit to Japan will reveal

Afterword

new layers of meaning in the phrases you've mastered, and you'll find joy in recognizing familiar words and expressions.

A Lasting Bond with Japan

The beauty of language is that it's a living, breathing entity that evolves with us. As you keep this book close, remember that it's not just about the words and phrases; it's about the friendships, memories, and stories that you'll create along the way. Japan is not just a place to visit; it's an experience to be lived, a culture to be absorbed, and a language to be loved.

As you close this book, know that the end of this journey is just the beginning of a lifelong relationship with Japan. May you carry the spirit of "和" (wa, harmony) in your heart, and may your adventures in Japan be filled with joy, understanding, and endless discoveries. ありがとう (Arigatou), and until our paths cross again in the Land of the Rising Sun.

Made in the USA
Coppell, TX
25 May 2024

32779626R00065